BLACK ARTISTS
IN THE UNITED STATES

BLACK ARTISTS IN THE UNITED STATES

An Annotated Bibliography of Books, Articles, and Dissertations on Black Artists, 1779–1979

LENWOOD G. DAVIS
AND
JANET L. SIMS

Foreword by
JAMES E. NEWTON

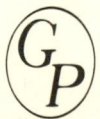

GREENWOOD PRESS
WESTPORT, CONNECTICUT • LONDON, ENGLAND

Library of Congress Cataloging in Publication Data

Davis, Lenwood G.
  Black artists in the United States.

  Includes index.
  1. Afro-American art—Bibliography.
2. Afro-American artists—Bibliography. I. Sims,
Janet, 1945-   joint author. II. Title.
Z5956.A47D38 [N6538.N5]   016.709'73   79-8576
ISBN 0-313-22082-4

Library of Congress Catalog Card Number: 79-8576
ISBN: 0-313-22082-4

First published in 1980

Greenwood Press
A division of Congressional Information Service, Inc.
51 Riverside Avenue, Westport, Connecticut 06880

Printed in the United States of America

10 9 8 7 6 5 4 3 2

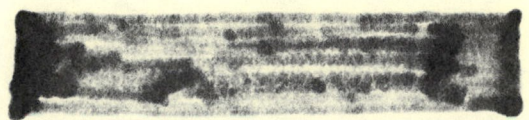

TO JAMES A. PORTER
"FATHER OF BLACK ART HISTORY"

Contents

Foreword

An important facet of America's early development was the role played by slave artisans and craftsmen. Slave art was an art of anonymity—an art that rose from slavery in the form of skilled handicrafts—an art descended from the remoteness of African imagery and later rechanneled as a functional aesthetic finding its way to the wrought-iron balconies of New Orleans, to the magnificent mansions of Charleston, South Carolina, and to the delicate furnishings and implements at Jefferson's Monticello. Receiving scant credit for his labor, the slave artisan and craftsman, through his artistic skill, provided the necessary workmanship of pre-industrial America and became the first class of "technocrats" in the new world. Early America was, indeed, fortunate to have the labors of Black craftsmen. Brought to the New World with the African legacy of involvement in the decorative arts, the Black handicrafters used their skills as producers of goods, builders, furniture makers, and designers of household objects and decor, thus aiding America in its aesthetic development. The creativity and ingenuity of the slave artisan class laid the foundation and provided the roots for furthering the development of the Afro-American artist.

While evidence is available indicating the slave artisans' role in laying the foundations of Afro-American art, much is still needed in the area of scholarship and research. Research for the study, investigation, and contributions of Black artists has been the focus of several historians and scholars, who have paved the way for developing and assessing the resources that are presently available to us. In 1940, Alain Leroy Locke, noted Afro-American art historian, scholar, and cultural philosopher, wrote in *The Negro in Art* that two major problems existed in exploring Afro-American art: (1) the "comparative inaccessibility to the materials"; and (2) the "prevalent impression that the fine arts . . . are less characteristic and less congenial mode of expression for the Negro. . . ." Other historians and art critics focused on Locke's viewpoint with similar perceptions. For example, James Porter, pioneer Afro-American art historian, in an address to the Association for the Study of Afro-American Life and History (Columbus, Ohio, 1941) comments:

> Whereas, studies of the Negro spiritual and the Negro folksong are plentiful, research has done very little to provide the student of culture with materials for criticism of folk and craft arts of the early Negro American.

In a more contemporary note Edmund B. Gaither reiterates much of Porter's and Locke's testimonies. Writing in the introduction of *Afro-American Artists: A Bio-Bibliographical Directory* (1943), Gaither maintains:

> In spite of his long and varied arts participation, the Black artist has not been integrated into the history of American art. Most books do not mention him at all and in others his citation is token and cursory. Even the popular interest in "Black art" and the "Black show" has done little to broaden the existing literature, and to stimulate art historical consideration of his work and plight.

Perhaps, as the literature indicates, the most discouraging element in reference to the Afro-American artist is the dearth of materials dealing specifically with Afro-American artworks. Until recently, much of the literature about Afro-American artists and their works has been limited to broad and general surveys with little, if any, information dealing with the experiential effects on the artists' lives. However, full-length books about Black artists, such as Horace Pippin, Henry O. Tanner, Romare Bearden, and others, are beginning to appear. Continuous efforts in this direction are of critical importance if the Afro-American artist is to take his rightful place in the history of American art.

In more recent years scholars have published volumes on Afro-American art—including Samella Lewis and Ruth Waddy's *Black Artist on Art, I and II* (1969); Judith Wragg Chase's *Afro-American Art and Craft* (1971); and David Driskell's *Two Centuries of Black American Art* (1976). Also of importance are recent doctoral dissertations by Lee Ransaw, Allan Gordon, Robert Spellman, John Clayton Moore, Hobie Williams, Walter Young, Althea Williams, Floyd Coleman, Oakley N. Holmes, Jr., and Murray DePillars, all of which are dealing specifically with Afro-American art.

In the works assembled here, Professor Lenwood G. Davis, a noted bibliographer and historian, and Janet Sims, a librarian at Howard University, have turned their abilities to bring together a host of books, articles, catalogs, reviews, and other resources to begin filling the informational void, which has so long been a nemesis when attempting to analyze and research the plight and role of artists of African descent.

The Davis-Sims bibliography is, indeed, refreshing when one notes the scarcity and paucity of available literature on the subject. The idea for the present volume was first generated by Dr. Davis, in September 1977, while a professor of Black American Studies at the University of Delaware. It was there that he, with the able assistance of Ms. Sims, began "collecting materials and resources to be utilized in developing a relatively definitive bibliography on the life and works of Afro-American artists."

Needless to say, the Davis-Sims team has produced a useful bibliographical tool that will be of paramount importance to all serious scholars of art, particularly students of Afro-American art. When any future history of Afro-American art is written, researchers will follow the broad guidelines of the work presented herein by Lenwood G. Davis and Janet Sims.

JAMES E. NEWTON
Director
Black American Studies

University of Delaware
Newark, Delaware
June 1979

Introduction

Currently there is a tremendous amount of attention given to the history of visual arts and artists in American society. Yet Black artists, as usual, are not included in those studies. The traditional reasons given for omitting Black artists are that they are a recent phenomenon and have made no historical artistic contributions to American society. Moreover, there is not enough available material on them. Since books, articles, and other materials are appearing regularly, few people can now say that there is not enough available material on them. As a matter of fact, James A. Porter, "The Father of Black Art History," wrote *Modern Negro Art* in 1943 and proved that Black artists not only have a long history of artistic contributions in the United States, but that they brought their art heritage here from Africa. Porter's pioneering study is still the classical work on Black art history. Alain Locke's *The Negro in Art,* that preceded Porter's work by three years (1940) also argued that Black people had a heritage of art in Africa before they came to the United States. The most recent study, Samella Lewis', *Art: African American* (1978), further supports Porter, Locke, and others' arguments that Black artists have a long tradition of art contributions to American society.

There were a number of Black artists even in the colonial period. Although Joshua Johnston (1765-1830) is generally recognized as the first "authenticated" Black American artist, another Black artist, Scipio Moorhead, was mentioned as a painter-slave during the 1770s. Phyllis Wheatley wrote a poem in 1773, "to S. M. [Scipio Moorhead], a young African Painter, on Seeing His Work." Although some writers have argued that Moorhead was only an amateur artist, nevertheless, he was recognized by his master's wife, Sarah Moorhead, for his ability. Mrs. Moorhead herself was a teacher of

art and no doubt instructed Scipio in the techniques of drawing and painting. From the colonial period to the present, a number of Black artists have
made significant contributions to art in America and had to fight to have
their works accepted by White artists and White society. These earlier
Black artists paved the way for the careers of Henry O. Tanner, Aaron
Douglass, Charles White, Romare Bearden, Hale Woodruff, Horace Pippin,
Augusta Savage, and other artists of African descent.

The Black artists, like some White artists, had to work at other jobs to
support themselves while painting. Unlike the White artists, however, Black
artists had the additional handicap of their color and their works not being
accepted by the larger society. Black artists' works have historically been
judged unfavorably by White critics. Consequently, their works were not
given the necessary exposure and were seldom reviewed in the White news
media, art magazines, and art journals. Moreover, their works were omitted
from major galleries and exhibitions. It is ironic that some Black American
artists had to go to Europe and elsewhere to have their works acclaimed
before they were recognized in the United States.

In compiling this volume, we have shown that there is sufficient evidence
to prove that Black artists have a long history of artistic contributions to
American society. This fact is just now becoming acceptable to the dominant
society. Hence, this bibliography should be useful for all those who want to
know more about the Black artists in the United States from colonial times
to the present.

This work is divided into six major sections. Section One deals with major
books on Black art. Since there are so few books on the subject, we gave
detailed annotations of them. Section Two entails general books. Although
these works did not deal specifically with Black art, they had a significant
section or chapter in them on the subject. Section Three discusses major
articles. We classified those articles as major that were ten or more pages in
length or several shorter ones written by the same author. Section Four
includes general articles. This is the largest section in the volume, for we
included not only articles in art journals, but also those from popular Black
periodicals, such as *Jet* and *Ebony,* as well as from earlier Black publications,
such as *Opportunity* and *Crisis.* Section Five depicts dissertations. Since
there were only a few, we gave in-depth attention to them. Section Six
lists Black artworks in the National Archives. The extensive index rounds
out this work and is most helpful in assisting the user of this bibliography.

We gratefully acknowledge the editorial and typing assistance that we
received from Ms. Eleana K. Smoot. She spent many laborious hours
typing and perfecting this manuscript to satisfy her high professional
standards. We would also like to thank the librarians at the Library of
Congress, Howard University, and Winston-Salem State University for
their assistance.

1
MAJOR BOOKS

1. Adams, Agatha Boyd. Contemporary Negro Arts. Chapel Hill, NC: University of North Carolina Press, 1948.

   There is only one section in this work that deals with visual art. The author is James Porter. He discusses the historical origins of Black art in the United States. Parts of this article have appeared elsewhere.

2. Albany Institute of History and Art. The Negro Artists Come of Age. Albany, NY: Albany Institute of History and Art, 1945.

   The title tells what this work is about. It also gives a survey of contemporary as well as earlier Black artists.

3. Alpha Kappa Alpha Sorority. Afro-American Women in Art: Their Achievements in Sculpture and Painting. Greensboro, NC: Alpha Kappa Alpha Sorority, December, 1969.

   The Afro-American women artists discussed in this thirty-two page booklet include Laura Wheeler Waring (1887-1948), Lois Mailou Jones, Eva Hamlin Miller, Elizabeth Catlett, Geraldine Hamilton McCullough, Emma Amos, Margaret Taylor Burroughs, Barbara Chase, Ethel Guest, Norma Morgan, Delilah Pierce, Lucille D. Robert, Jewel W. Simon, Bettye Saar, and Alma Thomas. Short bibliographic sketch of each artist is given. This work mentions that there are many young artists who have demonstrated their potential: Betty Blayton, Mildred A. Braxton, Ladybird Cleveland, Virginia Cox, Eugenia Dunn, Jane Hector, Esther Hill, Yvonne Hunt, and Mildred Thompson.

4. Atkinson, J. Edward, Editor. Black Dimensions in Contemporary American Art. NY: New American Library, 1971.

(Atkinson, J. Edward)

The fifty artists whose works appear in this volume are from every region of the United States. Their paintings represent a wide variety of styles and schemes which, in turn, reflect every trend in modern American art. The diversity of style, theme, and locale presented in this collection is unified by one immutable link---each artist is Black and living in the Twentieth Century America. There is a short bibliographical sketch of each author.

5. Barnett-Aden Collection. Washington, DC: The Barnett-Aden Gallery and The Smithsonian Institution Press, 1974.

The Barnett-Aden collection reflects the talents and concerns of a group of artists, many of whom are Black. The fact that this important Collection exists demonstrates, unquestionably, that even under the brutal and dehumanizing institution of slavery, the culture of Black people, transported across the vast waters, in the holds of slave ships, did not die. Some topics include: "Historical Notes," by Romare Bearden; "A Brief History of Afro-American Art," by Carolyn Margolis; "Thoughts of Black Art," "Tributes to the Founders of the Barnett-Aden Gallery," by Black artists Romare Bearden, Albert J. Carter, David C. Driskell, Sam Gillian, Carroll Greene, Jr., Jacob Lawrence, I. Rice Pereira, Lois Mailous Jones Pierre, Theodoros Stamos, Alma W. Thomas, James L. Wells, and Charles White. There is also a listing of Artists in the Collection and Selected Bibliography. There are one hundred twenty paintings and illustrations in this book.

6. Bearden, Romare and Harry Henderson. Six Black Masters of American Art. Garden City, NY: Doubleday & Co., 1972.

The six artists discussed are Joshua Johnston (17??-18??), Robert S. Duncanson (1822-1872), Henry Ossawa Tanner (1859-1937), Horace Pippin (1888-1946), Augusta Savage (1900-1962), and Jacob Lawrence (1917-   ). Short sketches are given of each artist as well as some of their works. There are also photos of the artists and an index. No bibliography is included.

7. Biggers, John and Carroll Simms. Black Art in Houston. College Station and London: Texas A & M University Press, 1948.

The title explains this work. Many of the paintings were by Biggers and Simms and some of their students at Texas Southern University. Besides paintings and illustrations, there are casein oil, tempera, terra

(Biggers, John and Carroll Simms)

cottas, bronze, and murals. Explanations are given concerning the background of most illustrations. No bibliography or index is included.

8. Bowdoin College Museum of Art. The Portrayal of The
Negro in American Painting. Brunswick, Maine: Bowdoin
College, 1964.

The title of this work explains what this exhibition is
about. Traditional artists such as Robert Duncanion and
Edmonia Lewis are included. There are also notes by
Sidney Kaplan that explain the significance of these
portrayals.

9. Brown, Milton W. Jacob Lawrence, NY: Whitney Museum
of American Art, 1974.

This was part of an exhibition of Jacob Lawrence's work
held at the Whitney Museum. The writer argues that
Jacob Lawrence was the first Black artist to be accepted so completely by what essentially is a White
art world. From the beginning, his art was not only
about Blacks, but represented them honestly without
idealization, sentimentality, or caricature. At the
same time, as a social realist, he considered the "struggle of man always to better his conditions and to move
forward . . . in a social sense." Brown concludes that
Lawrence has projected the Black experience in America
more consistently and effectively than any other Black
artist of his generation. He has at the same time continued to insist on the larger human struggle for freedom and social justice in all the world for all people.
There are fifty plates, six in color, and bibliography
included.

10. California Art Commission. The Negro in American Art.
Los Angeles: UCLA Art Galleries, Dickson Art Center,
1967.

This was an exhibition by the California Art Commission, UCLA Art Galleries, and Dickson Art Center. The
exhibition shows the contributions made by Black artists in America. There is also an essay by James A.
Porter, "One Hundred and Fifty Years of Afro-American
Art." Porter discusses the history of Black art in
America.

11. Cederholm, Theresa Dickson, Editor. Afro-American Artists. Boston: Boston Public Library, 1973.

The title explains what this book is about. This work
includes early artists such as Scipio Moorhead, thought
to be the first Black artist in America, Edward Mit-
chell Bannister (sometimes called Robert Bannister),

(Cederholm, Theresa Dickson, Editor)

Horace Pippin, and Romare Bearden as well as contemporary artists such as Samella Lewis, Ruth G. Waddy, and Charles White. Short bibliographical sketchs are given of each artist as well as their exhibits, awards, collections, publications, and sources. This work has an excellent bibliography of books, magazines, newspapers, and catalogues.

12.   Chase, Judith Wragg. Afro-American Art and Craft. NY: Van Nostrand Reinhold & Co., 1971.

The author discusses Black art and crafts from prehistoric Africa to contemporary times. She emphasizes the cultural history of Black art and attempts to bind various components together and show their relationships to each other. The author discusses the work of the pioneer Black artists of the Eighteenth and Nineteenth Centuries, and show their relationship to the mainstream of American art. She also takes a look at Black artists today, with special emphasis on their contributions to the contemporary craft renaissance. The writer used more than two hundred fifty paintings, drawings, photos, and illustrations to support her argument. A bibliography and index are included.

13.   City University of New York. The Evolution of Afro-American: 1800-1950. NY: City University of New York, 1967.

This work is based on an exhibition that was held at the City University of New York in 1967. More than forty paintings and illustrations are included. Short biographies of more than fifty artists and a list of their works are included. This work is broken down into different periods: "The Nineteenth Century," "The Negro Renaissance (1920s)," "The Depression Years - World War II," and "World War II - 1950." The works of the standard Black artists included: Joshua Johnston Hale Woodruff, Romare Bearden, and Charles White. Some Black sculptures are also included in this collection.

14.   Cornell University. Directions in Afro-American Art. Ithaca, NY: Herbert F. Johnson Museum of Art and The Africana Studies and Research Center, Office of University Publications, 1974.

This is a collection of Black artists' exhibitions that were held at Cornell University, September 18 through October 27, 1974. More than twenty-five artists and their works are included in this book. There are statements on art by many of the artists. Some of the artists include: Ralph Arnold, Kwasi Seitu Asantey, Suzzane Jackson, Marie Johnson, Valerie Maynard, Alfred J. Smith, Jr., Russ Thompson, Jack White, and Franklin

(Cornell University)

White. "Pioneers of Twentieth Century Afro-American
Art" and a "Selected Bibliography" are also included.

15.   Doty, Robert, Editor. Contemporary Black Artists in
      America. NY: Whitney Museum of American Art, 1971.

      The editor points out that ultimately the Black artist
      and his audience must respond to "the authority of the
      created thing," that unique quality which originates
      only with the creative individual, and which flourishes
      only under a spirit of free inquiry. The paintings in
      this book are part of an exhibition presented at the
      Whitney Museum, April 6 through May 16, 1971. There are
      more than forty paintings by the artists. A "Selected
      Bibliography" is also included.

16.   Driskell, David C. Amistad, II: Afro-American Art.
      Nashville, TN: Fisk University and United Church Board
      for Homeland Ministries, 1975.

      This is a collection of works that were on exhibition
      at Fisk University. The following topics are discussed:
      "The Amistad Incident," "The Afro-American Art: An In-
      side View," "The Phenomenology of a Black Aesthetic:
      Allan M. Gordon Interviews Himself." More than seventy-
      eight catalogues are listed. Most of the paintings dis-
      played at the exhibition are shown. There is also a
      "Selected Bibliography."

17.   _____. Two Centuries of Black American Art. NY:
      Los Angeles County of Art and Alfred A. Knopf, 1976.

      This is a collection of works that were on exhibition
      September 30 through November 21, 1976 through June 25
      through August 21, 1977. The following topics are dis-
      cussed: "Black Artists and Craftsmen in the Formative
      Years, 1750-1929," "The Evolution of a Black Aesthetic,
      1920-1950," "Index of Artists." There are brief bio-
      graphical sketches of each artist and some of his works.
      More than two hundred pictures and illustrations are in-
      cluded as well as a "Selected Bibliography."

18.   Fax, Elton C. Black Artists of the New Generation. NY:
      Dodd, Mead & Co., 1977.

      This work is an extension of an earlier book. Seventeen
      Black Artists, of the author. As its title suggests,
      it deals with mainly, but not exclusively, the younger
      post-depression artists; for it is they whose lives and
      works were so directly touched, and often seared, by the
      fiery turbulence of the 1950s and 1960s. There is a
      long discussion of each artist and his/her works. Of
      the twenty artists, nine are women. The artists dis-
      cussed are: Bertrand Phillips, Maurice Burns, Shirley

(Fax, Elton C.)

Stark, Alfred Ott Neals, Kay Brown, Alfred Smith, Jr.,
Onnie Rosalind Jeffries, John W. Outterbridge, Horathel
Hall, Leo E. Twiggs, and Dana Chandler. Photos of art-
ists and some of their works are also included.

19. _____. Seventeen Black Artists. NY: Dodd, Mead &
     Co., 1971.

     The seventeen Black artists include: Elizabeth Catlett,
     John Wilson, Lawrence Jones, Charles White, Eldzier
     Cortor, Rex Goreleigh, Charlotte Amenor, Romare Bearden,
     Jacob Lawrence, Roy De Carova, Faith Ringglold, Earl
     Hooks, James E. Lewis, Benny Andrews, Norma Morgan, John
     Biggers, and John Torres. The writer also discusses the
     "forerunners" of present day Black artists such as Josh-
     ua Johnston and Scipio Moorhead.

20. Feeling, Tom. Black Pilgrimage, NY: Lothrop, Lee and
     Shepard Co., 1972.

     This is the personal account of a Black American art-
     ist, Tom Feelings, who ultimately made a decision to
     leave the United States and live permanently in Africa-
     his ancestral home. A number of drawings and paintings
     by the author depict the various periods of his life.
     This book gives a rare insight into the evolution of
     Black consciousness. Feelings best summed up his
     thoughts when he declares "My heart is with the Black
     people in America, but my soul is in Africa."

21. Fine, Elsa Honig. The Afro-American Artist: A Search
     for Identity. NY: Holt, Rinehart & Winston, Inc.,
     1973.

     The author argues that from the arrival of Black people
     in North America, Blacks have been preoccupied with the
     creation of objects that possess aesthetic merit.
     Blacks, beginning in Colonial Times, produced some of
     the strongest and most original art to be seen in con-
     temporary America. Dr. Fine traces the Black artist
     from the colonial period to contemporary times. She
     concludes that until the 1960s, most Black art has been
     devoid of racial overtones and has conformed to the
     standards set by White academicians because Black art-
     ists did not want to offend Whites; therefore, they did
     not lead, or innovate, or ultimately make a significant
     contribution to American art. Hence, a system of segre-
     gation has confined the Black artist to a peripheral
     role in American art. This work includes more than
     three hundred forty paintings, illustrations, and
     photos, footnotes, bibliography, and index.

22. Frederick Douglass Institute. The Art of Henry O. Tanner
     1859-1937. Washington, DC: Frederick Douglass Insti-

(Frederick Douglass Institute)

tute in collaboration with the National Collection of
Fine Arts, Smithsonian Institution, 1970.

This small booklet is part of an exhibition held on
Tanner's works. This work includes: "Henry Ossawa
Tanner: Selections from His Writings," "Chronology of
Henry Ossawa Tanner (America, 1859-1937)," "Catalogue
of (His) Exhibition," "List of Awards," "List of Exhi-
bitions," "Photographs and Documents," "List of Organi-
zations," "Selected Bibliography," and "Index to Titles."
Nearly twenty of Tanner's paintings are included.

23. Gaither, Edmund B. Afro-American Artists. Boston:
Museum of Fine Arts, 1970.

This work includes short biographical sketches of eight-
een artists from Boston and fifty-one from New York.
Some of the artists from Boston include: Henry DeLeon,
Milton Johnson, Lois Mailou Jones, Gary Rickson, John
Wilson. Some of the artists from New York include:
Emma Amos, Benny Andrews, Romare Bearden, Betty Blayton,
Eldzier Cortor, Emilio Cruz, Jacob Lawrence, John W.
Rhoden, and Hale Woodruff. There is also a description
of their major works as well as the dimensions of them.

24. Harmon Foundation. Negro Artists: An Illustrated Review of Their Achievements. NY: Harmon Foundation,
Inc., 1935.

The title tells what this work is about. This work discusses "A Decade of Progress," "Art Study Through the
Workshop," and "News Notes on Negro Artists." A bibliographical sketch is given of artist Malvin Gray Johnson
and a number of his works are presented. Pictures and
prints of several of his works are shown. There is
also a "Directory of Negro Artists" including their ad-
dresses and their exhibitions.

25. Jones, Lois Mailou. Peintures, 1935-1951. Tourcoing,
France: Presses George Frere, 1952.

This work includes a portfolio of more than one hundred
plates detailing the artist's paintings. There is also
a biographical essay by James A. Porter. He discusses
the outstanding achievements of Jones.

26. _____. Reflective Moments. Boston: The
Museum of the National Center of Afro-American Artists,
1973.

A short biographical sketch of Lois Mailou Jones, one of
the most renown Black female artists in the United
States. She was born in 1905 in Boston and her works
have been exhibited in Europe as well as in the United

(Jones, Lois Mailou)

States.

27. Lewis, Samella S. and Ruth Waddy. Black Artists on Art.
Los Angeles: Contemporary Crafts, Inc., Publishers,
1971, Revised Edition, Vol. 1.

This book introduces the works and thoughts of more than
eighty-five producing Black American artists, including
the authors. This work according to the authors is a
book to promote change---change in order that art might
function as an expression rather than as an institution.
It could open many doors and many minds for it is varied
enough in its orientation to serve as a point of de-
parture for many avenues of expression. Photos and biographical sketches are included of each artist.

28. _____. Black Artists on Art. Los Angeles: Contemporary Crafts, Inc., Publishers, 1971, Vol. 2.

This volume is a follow up of Volume 1. Like the earlier work, it also introduces the works and thoughts of
Black American artists. More than seventy artists are
included. The writers hope that this book will speak
to the concept of nation building. They believe that
Black people must move on with the job of recording and
documenting, from their own perspectives, those of our
society, and indeed---of the world. Photos and biographical sketches are included of each artist.

29. _____. Art: African American. NY: Harcourt Brace
Jovanovich, Inc., 1978.

The book discusses the history of Black art in the
United States. The author surmises that Black art in
America had its origins in Africa and was transplanted
here. She argues that Black art is a reflection of the
Black experience. Lewis feels that inspite of oppression, Black people are a creative segment in American
society. This work also discusses the remnant of
Seventeenth Century slave handcrafts and proceeds
through the intervening centuries to the artistic ex-
plosion of the mid-Twentieth Century. There is a biographical sketch of each artist discussed. More than
two hundred fifty paintings, illustrations, drawings,
and sketches are included in this work. Some are in
color. An extensive Bibliography is also included.

30. Locke, Alain. Negro Art: Past and Present. Washington, DC: Associates in Negro Folk Education, 1936.

The writer discussed Black art in the United States beginning with Scipio Moorhead in 1773 and stopping with
the Black artists of the 1930s. Dr. Locke also discussed African art. The author concludes that the

(Locke, Alain)

Negro artist, needs the creation of a wide base of popular support from the people themselves, which again
depends on how rapidly and successfully the campaign
for the popularization of good art can be carried forward. There are also discussion questions and references at the end of each of the ten chapters.

31.   _____, Editor. The Negro in Art: A Pictorial Record
of Negro Artists and the Negro Theme in Art. Washington, DC: Associates in Negro Folk Education, 1940.

The title tells you what this work is about. Topics
discussed include: "The Negro As Artist," "The Negro
in Art," and "The Ancestral Arts." There are illustrations of the artist's works as well as biographical
indices of each artist. Locke argues that slaves
brought their skills as artists with them here to America from Africa. The editor concludes that we must not
expect the work of the Negro artist to be too different
from that of his fellow-artists. Product of the same
social and cultural soil, our art has an equal right
and obligation to be typically American at the same
time it strives to be typical and representative of
the Negro.

32.   _____, Editor. The New Negro: An Interpretation.
NY: Albert and Charles Boni, 1925.

There are two chapters that discuss Black art: "Negro
Art in America," by Albert C. Barnes and "The Legacy of
the Ancestral Arts," by Alain Locke. Barnes points out
that the contributions of the American Negro to art are
representative because they come from the hearts of the
masses of a people held together by yearnings and stir-
red by the same causes. He argues that Negro art is a
great art because it embodies the Negro's individual
traits and reflects their suffering, aspirations, and
joys during a long period of acute oppression and dis-
tress. Locke argues that Negro Americans got their
artistic influence from Africa. He concludes that if
even the vogue of African Art should pass, and the
bronzes of Benin and other African societies' works
should again become mere items of exotic curiosity,
for the Negro artists they ought still to have the importance and influence of classics in whatever art expression is consciously and representatively racial.

33.   Mandle, Roger, Editor. Thirty Contemporary Black Artists. Minneapolis: Minneapolis Institute of Arts,
1968.

These thirty Black artists' works were part of an exhibition held at the Minneapolis Institute of Arts, October 17 through November 24, 1968. Several of the art-

(Mandle, Roger)

ists make strong statements through their paintings
about the condition of Black Americans, and others
draw upon African art as a source of inspiration.
Generally, the artists are responding to the crosscur-
rents of contemporary art, and are primarily concerned
with recent experiments in form and technique, according to the editor. Some of the artists include: Romare
Bearden, Betty Blayton, Robert Gordon, Jacob Lawrence,
Norman Lewis, Bettye Saar, Emilio Cruz, Floyd Coleman,
Jack White, Edward Wilson, and Avel de Knight.

34. Mathews, Marcia M. Henry Ossawa Tanner: American Art-
     ist. Chicago: University of Chicago Press, 1969.

     This is the first biographical study of Henry Ossawa
     Tanner. The author gives the reader an insight into
     the art trends of the Nineteenth and early Twentieth
     Centuries and also into the struggle of Blacks in
     America at that time. Mathews concludes that Tanner
     will always have a special place in the minds and
     hearts of Black Americans because he was the first
     among them who with single-minded intensity pursued a
     path of excellence and rose superior to most of his
     White contemporaries in the highly conpetitive field of
     art. It is true that his success came first in Europe,
     and that he lived abroad most of his life, but despite
     his success and exile, he never lost his feeling of
     Americanism or his sense of identity with the Black
     race.

35. Miller, Samuel C., Editor. Black Artists: Two Genera-
     tions. Newark, NJ: The Newark Museum, 1971.

     This work combines a recreation of the Newark's Museum
     pioneering show with a survey of the paintings and
     sculpture being produced by today's Black artists in
     the New York-New Jersey areas. The collections in this
     booklet are part of an exhibition held in the Newark Mu-
     seum, May 13 through September 16, 1971. More than
     thirty-five contemporary artists' works were included
     in the exhibition. Some of them include: Romare
     Bearden, Barbara Fudge, Robert Knight, Don Miller, Rev.
     Arthur Roach, Margret Slade, and Hale Woodruff.

36. Parry, Ellwood. The Image of the Indian and Black Man
     in American Art: 1590-1900. NY: George Braziller,
     1974.

     The author argues that during the Seventeenth Century,
     pictures of Black slaves or servants in America were
     virtually nonexistent. The only Blacks in Colonial
     portraiture were household servants, endlessly waiting
     at the elbow of their White masters. Blacks were usual-
     ly forced to play comic parts in American geure scenes

(Parry, Elwood)

and political cartoons well into the 1800s, followed by
the Civil War Era and then Reconstruction, that images
of Black men began to change drastically in content as
they multiplied rapidly in number. Parry concludes that
burgeoning interest in the legal end of slavery and the
new life of the Blacks thereafter resulted in a major
reversal of roles.

37.   Patterson, Lindsay, Editor.   The Negro in Music and Art.
       NY: Publishers Co., 1969.

There is one section that deals with African and Black
Art: "Primitive Negro Sculpture and Its Influence on
Modern Civilization," "Negro's Art Lives in His Wrought
Iron," "The American Negro as Craftsmen and Artists,"
by James V. Herring, "The Negro Artist and Modern Art,"
by Vernon Winslow, "The Negro Art in Chicago," by Willard F. Motley, "Advance on the Art Front," by Alain
Locke, "The Harmon Awards," by Evelyn S. Brown, "Negro
Artists Gain Recognition After Long Battle," by James A.
Porter, "Four Rebels in Art," by Elton C. Fax, "Artists
of the Sixties," by Hale Woodruff, "Contemporary Artists," by Lindsay Patterson. There are a number of
short biographical sketches and illustrations of their
works which are included. The author concludes that
the Black artist today reflects increasingly the larger
society into which he is steadily moving. He is fortunate in that he has two distinct heritages to draw
upon, and he is learning rapidly to combine them, with
his own personal vision, into a universal statement concerning the total human experience.

38.   Porter, James, A.   Modern Negro Art.   With a new preface
       by the author, NY: Arno Press and The New York Times,
       1969.

The work remains the classical work on Black American
art although it first was published in 1943. The author,
an artist, traces Black art from (Pre-Civil War Days)
colonial times to the Twentieth Century. Porter argues
that the Black artist in America emerged from a background of folk art, and his formal speech was grounded
in the industrial idiom of the New World. The sphere
had been difficult, but historical evidence shows that
his crafts productions must have been considerable and
so suggests a future complete review, based on a search-
ing investigation into the whole body of American folk
art. This work contains ten chapters, Appendix (Memo-
rabilia of the Early Negro Artists), Notes, Bibliography, Index, and more than eighty drawings (halftone
plates).

39.   _____. Ten Afro-American Artists of the Nineteenth
       Century. Washington, DC: The Gallery of Art, Howard

(Porter, James A.)

University, 1967.

This is a catalogue prepared by Porter from an exhibition commemorating the centennial of Howard University, February 3 through March 30, 1967. The ten artists are: Joshua Johnston (ca. 1796-ca. 1824), Patrick M. Reason (1917-ca. 1850), Robert S. Duncanson (1817-1872), Eugene Warburg (ca. 1825-1867), Edward M. Bannister (1928-1901), Julian Hudson (Active ca. 1803-1840), Edmonia Lewis (1843-1900), William Simpson (Active ca. 1854-1872), Annie W. Walker (1855-1929), Henry Ossawa Tanner (1859-1937); A Selected Bibliography is included.

40.   _____. Afro-American Artists in the Nineteenth Century. Washington, DC: Howard University, 1967.

A short biographical sketch of several authors and a listing of their works and the person or organization lending the works. Several of their works are shown in black and white and A Selected Bibliography is included.

41.   Rodman, Selden. Horace Pippin: A Negro Painter in America. NY: Quadrangle Press, 1947.

A short, twenty-five biographical sketch of Horace Pippin, covering the years, 1888 to 1944. There are more than sixty paintings of the artist as well as an Appendix that includes: "My Life's Story by Horace Pippin," "Pippin's Life: A Brief Chronology," and a chronological and complete catalogue of Pippin's paintings in museums and private collections.

42.   _____ and Carole Cleaver. Horace Pippin: The Artist as a Black American. Garden City, NY: Doubleday & Co., 1972.

The writers contend that Pippin's pride in his race's struggle out of slavery and toward self-fulfillment is just as manifest. But these were only part of his pride in being an American, conclude the authors. The writers discuss the real meaning of many of Pippin's works. More than twenty-five illustrations by Pippin are included.

43.   Roelof-Lanner. T. V. Prints by American Negro Artists. 2d. ed., Los Angeles: Cultural Exchange Center of Los Angeles, 1967.

More than fifty-nine illustrations are included in this work. There is also an Introductory Essay by James A. Porter, "One Hundred Fifty Years of Afro-American Art."

(Roelof-Lanner)

Much of this information has appeared elsewhere.

44. Society of African Culture. Colloquim on Negro Art:
     First World Festival of Negro Arts, Dakar, April 1-24,
     1966. Dakar, Senegal: Society of African Culture,
     1968.

     There is one article,"Contemporary Afro-American Art,"
     by James A. Porter included in this work. He gives a
     historical overview of Afro-American art. He surmises
     that there is a cultural upsurage of crucial importance
     and it offers the artist and the writer unprecedented
     opportunities for the development of mobility and inde-
     pendence of creative thought and imagery. It is a chal-
     lenge to all his (Afro-American) capabilities though
     the answer to the query actually rests with the Negro
     people as a whole, not specifically with their inter-
     preters. Therefore, concludes Porter, it is predictable
     that only the as yet unspent social and cultural drives
     of that people can unfailingly sustain the Negro artist
     as he embraces the broader opportunities of the future.

45. Ten Negro Artists from the United States .
     NY: United States Committee for the First World Festi-
     val of Negro Arts, Inc. and The National Collection of
     Fine Arts, Smithsonian Institution, 1966.

     The artists and their works were present at the First
     World Festival of Negro Arts, Dakar, Senegal [Africa],
     1966. The ten artists include: Barbara Chase, Emilio
     Cruz, Sam Gilliam, Richard Hunt, Jacob Lawrence, Wil-
     liam Majors, Norma Morgan, Robert Reid, Charles White,
     and Todd Williams. There are short biographical
     sketches of each artist, and an illustration of each
     artist's work.

46. Thompson, Robert F. African Art and Afro-American Art:
     The TransAtlantic Tradition. NY: McGraw-Hill, 1968.

     The title tells what this work is about. The author
     points out that Black American art had its origins in
     Africa.

47. Washington, M. Bunch, with an introduction by John A.
     Williams. The Art of Romare Bearden: The Prevalence of
     Ritual. NY: Harry N. Abrams, Inc., Publishers, 1972.

     More than ninety drawings and paintings are included of
     Romare Bearden that he did between 1940- 1971. There
     is a biographical outline of the artist, listing of his
     exhibitions, a Selected Bibliography that include writ-
     ings by Romare Bearden, articles, and reviews of his
     works, exhibition groups and his one-man show, and exhi-
     bition catalogues of his works.

48.   White, Charles.   Images of Dignity: The Drawing of
       Charles White.   Los Angeles: W. Ritchie Press, 1967.

       The title explains this work. There is a Foreword by
       Harry Belafonte, Introduction by James Porter, and Com-
       mentary by Benjamin Horowitz. Porter, perhaps, best
       summed Charles White when he asserts: "I like to
       just think of Charles White not as an artist - nor even
       as an American artist - but as an artist, who, more than
       any other, has found a way of embodying in his art the
       very texture of Negro experiences as found in life in
       America. Charles is an artist steeped in life; and his
       informed artistic vision conduces to an understanding of
       vivid pictorial symbols which through large as life it-
       self, are altogether free of false or distorted ideas
       or shallow and dubious emotion." There are more than
       seventy-five drawings of White along with a short bio-
       graphical sketch of him and his accomplishments.

2
GENERAL BOOKS

49. Bardolph, Richard. The Negro Vanguard. NY: Vintage Books, 1961.

The writer briefly discusses eleven artists for the years 1900-1936: Henry O. Tanner, Aaron Douglas, William E. Scott, Archibald Motley, Edward A. Harleston, Palmer O. Hayden, Laura Wheeler Waring, James L. Wells, Malvin G. Johnson, Hale Woodruff, and Richmond Barthe. Bardolph argues that racial subjects before 1920, were virtually tabooed by potential White patrons; and yet the Black artist, thus diverted from themes he knew best, was censored for imitation and for stifling honest self-expression. The author suggests that in the 1920s the race-proud generation provided a rallying point for rebellion.

50. Baur, John I. H., et al., Editors. New Art in America: Fifty Painters of the Twentieth Century. NY: New York Graphic Society, 1957.

Jacob Lawrence is the only Black artist included in this work. The editors point out that Lawrence was at one time interested in theater scenery, and there is theater in his art in the best sense. Lawrence concludes that reality is not PRESENTED visually but CONVEYED visually by the simplest means, and it achieves our absolute belief.

51. Brawley, Benjamin. The Negro in Literature and Art in the United States. NY: Duffield & Co., 1930.

There is one chapter in this work that discusses Black artists. The writer discusses various painters beginning with Scipio Moorehead to Henry O. Tanner. The majority of the article is devoted to Tanner. Locke concludes that Tanner's whole career is a challenge and an inspiration to aspiring painters, and his work a monument of sturdy endeavor and exalted achievement.

52. Butcher, Margaret Just. _The Negro in American Culture_.
    NY: Alfred A. Knopf, 1972.

    One chapter is devoted to "Negro as Artist and in Ameri-
    can Art." The author discusses Black art in Africa and
    in America. She asserts that Edward Bannister was the
    first Black in America to receive real recognition as a
    painter and May Howard Jackson was the first Black art-
    ist to break away from academic cosmopolitanism and
    turn to frank and deliberate racism. Butcher argued
    that perhaps the art of Hughie Lee-Smith symbolizes the
    ultimate objective of Black artists. The author de-
    clares that we must not expect the work of the Black art-
    ist to be too different from that of his fellow artists.
    Product of the same social and cultural soil, the
    Blacks' art has an equal obligation to be typical and
    representative of the Blacks. The writer concludes
    that ultimately the Black American must make as dis-
    tinct a contribution to the visual art as he has made
    to music.

53. Cooper, William Arthur. _A Portrayal of Negro Life_. Dur-
    ham, NC: The Seeman Printery, 1936.

    According to the author "showing the real Negro through
    art is the primary purpose of this book." The author
    states that the second course led him to prepare this
    book of paintings is the interest in painting of
    Negroes shown by the two great races in America: Black
    and White. Another purpose of this work was to portray
    some phase or moods of Negro life. There are twenty-
    seven paintings. Some of the titles include: "The Van-
    ishing Washerwoman," "The Old Cook," "The Shoe Shine
    Boy," "A Negro's Conception of Christ in the Life To-
    day," and "A Modest Negro Beauty." There are short
    biographical sketches of each painting.

54. Davis, John P., Editor. _The American Negro Reference
    Book_. Englewood Cliffs, NJ: Prentice-Hall, Inc., 1966.

    There is one chapter in this work, "The Negro in the
    Fine Arts," by Marion Brown. The author gives a histo-
    rical overview of Black art in the United States from
    colonial times to the 1960s. He argues that near the
    beginning of the Nineteenth Century, there were many
    free Black artists who earned their living at other jobs
    while painting in their spare time. Brown points out
    that the period of Black art until the emergence of
    Henry O. Tanner may be styled "the apprentice period,"
    and covered roughly from 1865 to 1890. From 1890 until
    near 1914, the Black artist advanced from apprentice to
    journeyman. The writer concludes that the future of
    the Black artist in America is now almost solely limited
    only by his or her ability to create. Many Blacks go to
    Europe, but not so much for environmental freedom as for
    the benefits of seeing and feeling the cosmopolitan at-

(Davis, John P.)

titudes which Europe has always had for the arts and
artists.

55. Diop, Alioune, Editor. <u>Africa as Seen by American
     Negroes</u>. Paris, France: Presence Africaine, 1958.

     There is one chapter in this work by James A. Porter,
     "The Transcultural Affinities of African Negro Art,"
     that discusses art. He contends that African art had a
     direct influence on the folk arts of the Negroes in the
     United States. Porter concludes that Negroes in America
     should hold onto their many vestiges of their African
     heritage no matter how much despised by others.

56. Gayle, Addison, Jr., Editor. <u>The Black Aesthetic</u>. Gar-
     den City, NY: Doubleday & Co., 1971.

     Three articles in this book of essays are devoted to
     Black art and artists: John O'Neal, "Black Arts: Note-
     book," Langston Hughes, "The Negro Artists and the Ra-
     cial Mountain," and Larry Neal, "The Black Art Movement."
     Mr. O'Neal states that when Black art happens, it is
     different. He concludes the affirmation of the Black
     reality, not contradiction and denial. Affirmation of
     Black potential, not trying to take Black dreams and
     paint them white till even we don't know the difference
     anymore. Black life is the model. Hughes argues that
     Black artists must not be ashamed to paint Black themes.
     An artist must be free to choose what he does, certainly,
     but he must never be afraid to do what he might choose.
     Mr. O'Neal believes that the Black Art Movement is radic-
     ally opposed to any concept of the artist that alienates.

57. Goldstein, Rhoda L. <u>Black Life and Culture in the
     United States</u>. NY: Thomas Y. Crowell Co., 1971.

     There are two chapters in this book that deal with
     Black American art: "Black Artists in the United
     States," by James Denmark and "Is Black Art About Col-
     or?," by Frank Bowling. Denmark gives an overview of
     Black artists in America from Robert M. Douglas, Jr.,
     to Benny Andrews. He points out that most Blacks have
     to earn their living at other jobs while painting. He
     concludes that many Black artists are going to Africa to
     try to bridge, somehow, that time gap; to try to rein-
     force and regenerate the creative power that was lost
     by time, by slavery, by the breaking up of families,
     by the by the breaking up of groups. Bowling attempts
     to answer the question, Is Black art to be appraised
     for its Blackness or its artistic merit? The author
     believes that some Black artists are being judged by
     their artistic merits. Bowling concludes that should
     works of paintings continue to be a Black issue and not
     an art issue these works will suffer.

58. Grigsby, J. Eugene, Jr. Art and Ethnic: Background for Teaching Youth in a Pluralistic Society. Dubuque, Iowa: William C. Brown Company Publishers, 1977.

Chapters two and seven discuss Black art. The writer discusses the historical evolution of Black art history from the 1940s to the 1970s. A number of major Black exhibitions are mentioned. The author gives quite a bit of Black history beginning with the arrival of the first slaves in America to the 1970s. The writer points out that Black artists used history in illustrating their works. Many Black artists also used art as a means of protesting against injustice in American society.

59. Huggins, Nathan Irvin, Editor. Voices From the Harlem Rennaisance. NY: Oxford University, 1976.

There are two sections in this book that deal with Black art: Alain Locke, "The Legacy of the Ancestral Art," and "Visual Arts: To Celebrate Blackness." Locke points out that Black American art had its origins in African art. The latter article discusses eight artists and their works: Aaron Douglas, Sargent Johnson, Richmond Barthe, Augusta Savage, Hale Woodruff, William H. Johnson, Archibald J. Motley, and Palmer Hayden.

60. Newton, James E. and Ronald L. Lewis. The Other Slaves: Mechanics, Artisans, and Craftsmen. Boston: G. K. Hall, 1978.

There are three chapters in this book that discuss Black artists: "The Negro as Artist," by Alain Locke, "Negro Craftsmen and Artists of Pre-Civil War Days," by James A. Porter, and "Slave Artisans and Craftsmen: The Roots of Afro-American Art," by James E. Newton. The earlier two articles by Locke and Porter were taken from their two books and have appeared elsewhere in this annotation. The latter one by Newton is an original article. He argues that the roots of slave artisans and craftsmen had their origins in Africa and they brought it to America. Newton concludes that Black artisans and craftsmen constituted a specialized labor force in Colonial America; without their achievements it is difficult to see how the colonists would have survived.

61. Ploski, Harry A., Editor. Reference Library of Black America. NY: Bellwether Publishing Co., Inc., 1971. Book IV.

Chapter Two discusses Black artists. The author argues that Black artists are demanding no more than formal exposure and the opportunity to break through the facade of formal custom which has prevented them from even attempting to become more creative individuals. He concludes, this achieved, the art world may finally be able

(Ploski, Harry A.)

boast of parity between its Black and White members.
More than thirty-seven painters, sculptors, ceramists,
and their biographical sketches are included in this
work.

62. Porter, James A. "The Negro in Modern Art." in The New
     Negro: Thirty Years Afterward. Papers Contributed to
     the Sixteenth Annual Spring Conference of the Division
     of Social Sciences, April 20-22, 1955. Washington, DC:
     Howard University, Graduate School, 1955.

     Porter notes that Dr. Alain Locke recognized a call to
     duty in essaying criticism and guidance of the Black
     artist. He wrote three books and numerous articles on
     Black art as well as the foreword to several art exhi-
     bition catalogues. He cites the era of the New Negro
     as one of the new directions for the Black artist. The
     double standard of appraisal and employment was disap-
     pearing, but the Black artist is still required to be
     judged as seriously, as continually, and as construc-
     tively as any other artist; and he also required a dis-
     criminating, consistent and generous patronage.

63. Robinson, Armstead, et al., Editors. Black Studies in
     the University: A Symposium. New Haven, CT: Yale
     University Press, 1969.

     There is one chapter that discusses Black art: "African
     Influence on the Art of the United States," by Robert
     Farris Thompson. The writer argues that contrary to
     general opinion, important Afro-American influenced
     art exists in the United States. Thompson lists seven
     traits common to most United States Afro-American art
     that suggest African influences. The author concludes
     that "mankind must applaud Afro-American art in the
     United States for its sheer existence, a triumph of
     creative will over forces of destruction."

64. Rogers, J. A. World's Great Men of Color. NY: J. A.
     Rogers, 1947, Vol. II.

     The author argues that throughout all of his paintings,
     Henry O. Tanner shows a profound thoughtfulness, a pene-
     trating psychology, and a nature truly poetic. The
     strength of his imaginative sense is perhaps best reveal-
     ed by his use of color. The writer concludes that al-
     though his paintings exhibit that full-blooded sense of
     rhythm which gives a peculiar charm to the art produc-
     tions of his race, Tanner's work is above all racial dis-
     tinctions. He should no longer be classed as the fore-
     most Negro painter, but rather, as one of the greatest
     artists America has produced.

65.   Roucek, Joseph S. and Thomas Kiernan. _The Negro Impact on Western Civilization_. NY: Philosophical Library, 1970.

There is one section in this work by James A. Porter, "Contemporary Black American Art." The author discusses Black art with its beginnings in Africa to contemporary (1960s) America. He points out that in America, the racial double standard operates in the field of art as in other fields of endeavor. Porter surmises that there are material gains in the forms of prizes, awards, commissions, honors, and sales of which some Black artists, particularly those of wide reputation, have had their share. The writer concludes that it is predictable that only the as yet unspent social and cultural drives of that people (Whites) can unfailingly sustain the Black artist as he embraces the broader opportunities of the future.

66.   Smythe, Mabel A. _The Black American Reference Book_. Sponsored by the Phelps-Stokes Fund. Englewood Cliffs, NJ: Prentice-Hall, 1976.

Chapter 26 discusses "Afro-American Art," by Edmund B. Gaither. The writer gives an historical overview of Afro-American art. He contends that the visual-arts tradition of Black America can be most fully appreciated if the art is approached in terms of social history. Social circumstances have affected Black artists' abilities to participate in the mainstream of American art much more than have their White counterparts. Gaither believes that subject matter, style, patronage, and work arena have at every point been affected by their dubious standing as artists, Americans, and human beings. The author concludes the advocates of the Afro-American artist should by the very presence, help to free the artist to devote himself to his art. In the past, the Afro-American artist had to serve as his defender, advocate, and critic.

67.   Toppin, Edgar A. _A Biographical History of Blacks in America Since 1528_. NY: David McKay Co., Inc., 1971.

Short biographical sketchs are given of five artists: Edward M. Bannister (1821-1901), Robert Ducanson (1817-1972), Henry O. Tanner (1859-1937), Charles White (1918-), and Hale Woodruff (1900-   ).

68.   Whiting, Helen Adele with Illustrations by Lois Mailou Jones. _Negro Art, Music and Rhyme for Young Folk_. Washington, DC: Associated Publishers, Inc., 1938.

The artist did a number of illustrations on African and Black American life. The author points out that any child or adult should have greater respect for the Negroes contributions to society after having read

(Whiting, Helen Adele)

these simple direct stories-as simple, and direct as
African art itself.

3
MAJOR ARTICLES

69. Andrews, Benny. "A Gallery with All the Comforts of Home." _Encore_, Vol. 5, June 21, 1976, pp. 30-31.

Peg Alston had made her New York apartment into an art gallery. She first became a collector and then an art dealer. Her home gallery includes works by Ed Clark and Romare Bearden.

70. _____. "The B.E.C.C. - Black Emergency Cultural Coalition" _Art_, Vol. 44, Summer, 1970, pp. 18-20.

In criticism of the poor handling of the Black "Harlem on Mu Mind" Exhibition at the Metropolitan Museum of Art, a group formed the Black Emergency Cultural Coalition to fight racism in the cultural area of American society and serve as a watchdog group for the Black community in the graphic arts.

71. _____. "Black Artists Getting It On." _Encore_, Vol. 4, August 18, 1975, pp. 42-44.

Andrews discussed the renaissance of Black cultural awareness and names of some of the Black artists: Jonathan Bruce, Beverly Buchanan, Kay Brown, Leslie Price, James Phillips, J. D. Jackson, and Cleveland Bellows.

72. _____. "Black Artists Say, Give Us More Space." _Encore_, Vol. 4, December, 1974, p. 45.

Mr. Andrews spoke of the problems of Black artists and White critics and how publications, especially Black ones, fail to devote space to Black art and Black art critics. He also talks about how he decided to set up a panel on "A Confrontation Between Black and White Critics" after the editor of _Art Forum_ failed to deal with the problem of Black art and Black art critics.

73. Andrews, Benny. "JAM Opens in New York." Encore, Vol.
     4, April 7, 1975, p. 24.

     The JAM (Just-Above Mid-town) Gallery opened in New
     York in November, 1974. The gallery handled works
     exclusively by Black artists and would feature the
     works of twelve artists plus other artists not under
     contract to the gallery. The gallery was founded and
     directed by twenty-five year old Linda Bryant. A pic-
     ture of Suzanne Jackson, one of the gallery artists,
     and a scene of the opening are included.

74. _____. "Jemimas, Mysticism, and Majos: The Art of
     Bettye Saar." Encore, Vol. 4, March 17, 1975, p. 30.

     Ms. Saar was to have an exhibit of her works at the
     Whitney Museum in New York. Her works consist of
     codes and secrets. The artist's earlier works con-
     tained images of the occult, palmistry, and astrology.
     Then she went into African fetishes, mojos, and boxes
     containing organic and natural materials. She went
     later into Black imagery where she used derogatory
     figures (Uncle Toms and Aunt Jemimas) and related them
     to the Black Liberation Movement, such as Aunt Jemima
     holding a gun. Her latter works are more subtle and
     less violent. In her use of framing her pictures in
     window boxes, she explained that the window was a way
     of traveling from one conscious level to another and
     boxes represent a kind of secret that can open and
     close at will.

75. _____. "Major Art Publications Excludes Blacks."
     Encore, Vol. 4, May 5, 1975, p. 44.

     The author notes how most art books either totally ig-
     nore the influence of African art or merely give it a
     brief mention. According to some authors, Black art
     has been covered and books dealing with Black art have
     already been published. Three examples of Black art
     are shown.

76. _____. "Positive Pull for Black Arts." Encore,
     Vol. 4, February 3, 1975, p. 38.

     The Elma Lewis Center is an umbrella of the National
     Center of Afro-American artists. The museum is ac-
     quiring a permanent art collection and has exhibited
     the works of major Black artists. The center also has
     other types of cultural activities. A biographical
     sketch of Ms. Lewis is given. A dancer and actress,
     she searches for the new ways to better the role of
     the artist and holds a vanguard role as a contributor
     and supporter of Black art.

77. _____. "Raymond Saunders: An Artist's Artist."
     Encore, Vol. 4, April 21, 1975, p. 35.

(Andrews, Benny)

Notes the article Saunders wrote in Arts Magazine in 1967 and how the article helped Black artists in a time when Black artists were trying to break into American art establishments. Saunders'work incorporates every-day objects: baggage, labels, chewing gum wrappers, theater stubs, etc. He feels that in order to get more exposure of works, artists should not let all of their works be exhibited publicly after they are sold. A picture of Mr. Saunders is shown.

78. _____. "The Street Artistry of Dana Chandler." Encore, Vol. 5, September 20, 1976, pp. 32-33.

Dana Chandler (Akin Duro) held an exhibit at Northeast-ern University. A street artist, he paints Black life. The Blackness he paints did not come out until 1967 when a riot in Boston produced much police brutality. He mostly paints murals and has given a lot of free art to Blacks. A picture of Chandler with some of his works and one painting, "Fred Hampton's Door," is shown.

79. _____. "The Huffs, Pilgrims Who Search and Find." Encore, Vol. 5, October 18, 1976, p. 32.

James and Ernestine Huff travel from city to city doing exhibits of their art. James is a more mature painter and is best when he is dealing with people. They have done exhibits at Houston's Contemporary Art Museum in Harlem. A picture of Mr. and Mrs. Huff is shown plus one of his paintings, "Mother of Civilization."

80. _____. "There's A Mural to this Story." Encore, Vol. 7, September 18, 1978, pp. 30-31.

Since its beginning as a form of social protest in 1967, urban Black muralism has become an acceptable form of art. The National Endowment for the Arts matches funds for murals and other public art projects. Subject matter has changed over the years as some corporations will not fund political or social murals. This article also looks at what the Black muralists are doing now. Two murals are shown.

81. Bowling, Frank. "Black Art III." Arts Magazine, Vol. 44, December, 1969/January, 1970, pp. 20-22.

Cites the criticisms of various writers on Black art. Mr. Bowling felt that the total thrust of the establish-ment toward annihilation by ignoring contemporary Black existence.

82. _____. "Discussion on Black Art." Arts Magazine, Vol. 43, April, 1969, pp. 16, 18, 20.

(Bowling, Frank)

The writer attempts to explain why the Black artist
has contributed so little to the most relevant aspects
of contemporary art. He writes about the works of
Black artists, Bob Thompson and Jack Whitten and discusses some of the dilemmas the Black artist faces in
gaining recognition for his works. This critique on
Black art shows the problems of both the older and
younger Black artists and attempts to find out if there
is such a thing as Black art. A painting by Mr. Thompson is shown.

83.   _____. "It's Not Enough to Say Black is Beautiful."
Art News, Vol. 70, April, 1971, pp. 53-55, 82-85.

Mr. Bowling discusses the problems of how to judge
Black art by Black artists. He examines the works of
William Williams, Al Loving, Dan Johnson, and Jack
Whitten. All of these artists have varying backgrounds
and styles.

84.   _____. "The Rupture: Ancestor Worship, Revival,
Confusion, or Disguise." Arts Magazine, Vol. 44, Summer, 1970, pp. 31-34.

Author comments on negative comparisons in art criticism. Mr. Bowling feels that quality is the only cri-
terion from which to judge. Highly technical article
on how museums select exhibits and exactly what is an
all-Black exhibit and tells of the opening of several
art shows in New York and Boston.

85.   Cureau, Harold G. "The Historic Roles of Black American Artists: A Profile." Black Scholar, Vol. 9, No.
3, November, 1977, pp. 2-13.

The writer contends that Black artists are first and
foremost products of their unusual American experiences
as Black people. While Black artists are inextricably
a part of an ongoing struggle for full equality, they
must bear the added task of their thrust for full
recognition of their contributions to society as creative personalities. He concludes that the future en-
largement and extension of the roles of Black artists
will be considerably influenced in part by the willing-
ness of American society and its cultural agencies to
continue to make possible the acceptance and recognition of these artists, and the active concern and inter-
vention of Black controlled agencies, such as business-
es, to increase their support and encouragement of
Black artists.

86.   Greene, Carroll, Jr. "Perspective: The Black Artist
in America." Art Gallery, April, 1970, pp. 1-29.

(Greene, Carroll, Jr.)

Author notes that until recently a group show by Black
artists was a rarity. He gives biographical information on such Black artists as Edward Bannister, Henry
O. Tanner, and Joshua Johnston. He gave information on
such Black owned art galleries as the Barnes-Aden Gallery. Fifty-nine paintings by fifty-three artists
are shown.

87. "Leading Negro Artists," Ebony, September, 1963, pp.
    131-140.

The artists discussed in this article are: Jacob
Lawrence, Hale Woodruff, Charles Alston, Romare Beard-
en, Aaron Douglas, Norman Lewis, Richmond Banthe,
Richard Hunt, Charles White, John Biggers, Eldzier,
Palmer Hayden, John Rhoden, Selma Burke, and Hughie
Lee-Smith. These artists were selected by veteran
artist Hale Woodruff. This article contends that
America's leading Negro artists have demonstrated their
mastery of the full range of artistic expression, from
the conventional representational to the ultra modern
abstract.

88. Locke, Alain. "Advance on the Art Front." Opportun-
    ity, Vol. 17, May, 1939, pp. 132-136.

Talks about the many shows which have been staged
honoring Negro artists. He notes the support of the
Federal Art Project in helping Negro artists. Such
places and groups as the Harlem Artists Guild and ACA
Gallery have displayed the works of such artists as
Aaron Douglas, Augusta Savage, Jacob Lawrence, and
others. He notes the highly successful one-man show
at the Baltimore Museum of Art by Richard Barthe.
Locke lists artists of note plus places and groups
which helped support the Negro artists. Two paintings
and four sculptures are shown.

89. _____. "The American Negro As Artist." American
    Magazine of Art, Vol. 23, September, 1931, pp. 210-220.

Author notes that the American Negro artist is completely different from his African prototype. He cites
slavery as the historical reason because it cut him off
from his roots. The Negro then developed other skills
such as singing. He also gives a historical overview
of the achievements of Negroes in art, listing such
people as Henry O. Tanner, Meta Warrick Fuller, and
May Howard Jackson, to name a few. Since 1915, the
goal of the Negro artist was to project art that expressed the racial spirit and background plus show the
individual skill of the artist. Twelve works of art
by ten artists are shown.

90.   Locke, Alain.   "Beauty Instead of Ashes."   Nation, Vol.
       126, April 18, 1928, pp. 432-434.

       Dr. Locke speaks of all forms of art in this article.
       He feels that the Negro artist is effective in express-
       ing Negro life in the more subjective terms of poetry
       and music.   The author states that it is primarily be-
       cause Negro life is creatively flowing in American art
       and that it is the business of the Negro artist to cap-
       italize on it in his work.

91.   _____.   "Chicago's New Southside Art Center."   Maga-
       zine of Art, Vol. 34, August, 1941, pp. 370-374.

       The author notes the establishment of a well-equipped
       and publicly supported art center, the Southside Com-
       munity Art Center in Chicago.   The artists in the cen-
       ter had a chance to communicate their art, many exhi-
       bits were held there as well as classes.   In essence,
       this article tells what one community was doing to
       further the purpose of Black art.   Five paintings by
       various artists were shown plus three of the art center
       itself.

92.   _____.   "To Certain of Our Phillistines."   Opportun-
       ity, Vol. 3, May, 1925, pp. 155-156.

       The writer argues that the Negro painter has never
       maturely touched the portrayal of the Negro subject.
       He feels that art must discover and reveal the beauty
       which prejudice and caricature have obscured.   The
       artistic expression of Negro life must break through
       the stereotypes in order to be truly expressive.

93.   _____.   "Negro Art In America."   Design, Vol. 44,
       December, 1942, pp. 12-13.

       Professor Locke states that the aim of an exhibit on
       Negro artists is to acquaint the public with the works
       of the artists and to serve as a principal of what art
       should and must be.   The Negro theme and its develop-
       ment are part of the movement toward the use of nara-
       tive materials and subject matter.   He also notes the
       help of the Harmon Foundation and the Federal Art Pro-
       ject in sponsoring exhibits and broadening the apprecia-
       tion of art.   Two paintings are shown.

94.   _____.   "Negro's Contribution in Art to American
       Culture."   Proceedings of the National Conference of
       Social Work, May 15-21, 1932, pp. 315-322.

       The writer contends that Black art is a psychological
       index of the attitude of a select section of the race
       toward its own traits---physical, social and cultural.
       He discusses the accomplishments from the 1850s to the
       1930s.   Dr. Locke concludes that in the technical re-

(Locke, Alain)

lease and stepping up of creative energy latent in the
Black, the fine arts have a vital and valuable impetus
and yield toward the flowering of native and original
American fine arts.

95.   _____. "The Negro in Art." Association of American
Colleges Bulletin, Vol. 17, November, 1931, pp. 359-
364.

This address before the Tenth Annual Conference of the
International Student Service Committee talks about all
phases of Negro art. He defines Negro art as the inter-
action of American factors on the Negro. The author
notes the new interest in Negro art-the Negro Renais-
sance-with a new evaluation of the Negro in American
life. This new Negro Renaissance has the Negro emphasis with pride in his cultural heritage.

96.   Newton, James E. "Slave Artisans and Craftsmen: The
Roots of Afro-American Art." Black Scholar, Vol. 9,
November, 1977, pp. 35-42.

The author looks at the role played by slave/artisans
and craftsmen from its African origins to the 1860s.
Dr. Newton notes the facts surrounding the development
of these slave/artisans class. To meet the demand of
industrialism, more slaves were employed in all skills
in order to maintain the rise of plantation manufactur-
ing. There is also a list of the various occupations
held by Black artisans and craftsmen, plus a good bibliography.

97.   Pleasants, J. Hale. "Joshua Johnston: The First
American Negro Portrait Painter." Maryland Historical
Magazine, Vol. 37, No. 2, June, 1942, pp. 1-29, 77.

Some biographical information is given and the author
cites the problems in trying to find out if he had
been a slave and his correct name. This article lists
the subject, date, size, description, ownership, at-
tribution, and reproductions of his works. There are
eleven pictures included and covers the period 1789-
1825. Johnston is also compared to other artists:
Charles White, Willson Peale, etc.

98.   Porter, James A. "Art Reaches the People." Opportunity, Vol. 17, December, 1939, pp. 375-376.

The writer comments on the artistic interests of the
Negro masses in learning opportunities in the craft
arts. He praises the Federal Arts Project which as-
sisted in the development of artists by providing
training opportunities and sponsoring studios. The
few criticisms were that some programs set up especial-

(Porter, James A.)

ly for Negro artists were not continued long enough
to be effective and that the best teachers were not
secured to train Negro artists, nor were facilities
for training widely distributed to the Negro.

99.   . "Four Problems in the History of Negro
Art." Journal of Negro History, Vol. 27, January,
1942, pp. 9-36.

The four problems Porter discusses are: (1) the reality of handicrafts and fine arts by Negroes prior to
1820. Slaves were not given credit for their work;
(2) the Negro artists' relation to the mainstream of
American society; (3) the decline in the productivity
among Negro artists between 1870-1890 during the
period of Reconstruction and; (4) the period 1900-
1920 was actually the culmination rather than the beginning of an era of self expression for the Negro.
The author also discusses such artists as Henry O. Tanner, William H. Harper, Meta Warrick Fuller, and Laura
Wheeler Waring.

100.   . "Malvin Gray Johnson, Artist." Opportunity,
Vol. 13, April, 1935, pp. 117-118.

Porter pays tribute to Malvin G. Johnson. He notes
that his early death ended a brilliant career. His
best painting was done between 1931 and 1934. He became an experimentalist, first with color and then
with deeper problems of form. Shortly before his
death, he completed a series of canvasses depicting
genre aspects of Negro urban and rural life. They
were among the best painted records of contemporary
Negro types of social life. A picture of Mr. Johnson
at work is shown.

101.   . "Negro Art on Review." American Magazine
of Art, Vol. 27, January, 1934, pp. 33-38.

An exhibition by Negro artists at the National Museum
of the Smithsonian Institution was sponsored by the
Association for the Study of Life and History. It included works by students, amateurs, and professionals.
The exhibit indicated some of the stages in the development of the artists. The major part of the works
done by college students had a racial interest. Six
pieces by various artists are shown plus three pieces
from the students are included. Descriptions of the
art works of the artists are also given.

102.   . "Robert S. Duncanson-Midwestern Romantic-
Realist." Art in America, Vol. 39, October, 1951,
pp. 99-154.

(Porter, James A.)

This entire issue is devoted to the life of Robert S. Duncanson who was an acclaimed Black artist before the Civil War. Born in 1817, he worked both in the United States and abroad. Subject areas include a biography of the artist, the early paintings, years of transition, the portraits, the final paintings, a checklist of located and unlocated paintings, and a bibliography.

103.   _____. "Robert S. Duncanson." _Art in America_, Vol. 42, October, 1954, pp. 220-221, 235.

The writer notes that some lost paintings of Robert S. Duncanson has lengthened the list of his extant works, but not much more of his personal life and career has been found. It is known that he spent most of his life in Cincinnati, Ohio and some of his correspondence with Lunius Sloane is in the Newberry Library. These letters give some references to his personal philosophy of art, his methods of work, and lists the titles of some of his works, his patrons, and commissions.

104.   _____. "The Negro Artists and Racial Bias." _Art Front_, Vol. 3, June/July, 1937, pp. 8-9.

Porter discusses the techniques used by the segregationists and racialists in hindering the growth of the Black artists. These include the disbelief in the native craft arts as aspects of Negro culture, urging the Negro artists to adopt the forms used by the African artists, ignoring the contributions of Negro artists during the Eighteenth and Nineteenth Centuries. The author argues that the Negro must rely upon individual and environmental factors to determine the nature of real contributions to American culture. Porter concludes the article by discussing the problems facing Negro artists.

105.   Powell, Richard J. "I Too, Am America, Protest, and Black Power: Philosophical Continuities in Prints by Black Americans." _Black Art_, Vol. 2, Spring, 1978, pp. 4-5.

Twenty-three prints are shown with interpretations for each. A bibliography is included. The prints show expressions of unity, dissent, and independence and communicate some of Black America's most deeply felt attitudes and concerns.

106.   Reddick, Lawrence D. "Walter Simon: The Socialization of An American Negro Artist." _Phylon_, Vol. 15, 4th Quarter, 1954, pp. 373-392.

(Reddick, Lawrence D.)

A biographical sketch of Walter A. Simon, Jr. who won
the main prize at the Atlanta University Art Show in
1953. It also included biographical sketches of his
parents, his life in Brooklyn, and Harlem. While in
high school he attended afternoon classes at Pratt
Institute and had already won prizes for his art work.
He then went to the Academy of Fine Arts and graduated
in 1937. After his release from the United States
Army in 1945, he went to college where he met Hale
Woodruff who had a profound effect on his career.
Simon then went on to teach at Savannah State College
and Virginia State College where he was known as a
creative artist and a natural teacher.

107. Robinson, Louie. "Charles White: Portrayer of Black
     Dignity." Ebony, Vol. 22, July, 1967, pp. 25-28, 30,
     32, 34-36.

     Charles White's paintings, charcoal, and ink drawings
     are on display in museums and universities throughout
     the United States and in South America, the USSR,
     Poland, China, Hungary, Germany, and Czechoslovakia.
     His works are also in private art collections in
     Europe, Japan, India, Brazil, Africa, and Canada.
     Harry Belafonte said of Mr. White's work: "There is
     a powerful, sometimes violent beauty in his artistic
     interpretation of Negro Americana." The writer gives
     a biographical sketch in which twenty-six pictures of
     his work and ten of his works are shown.

108. Rose, Barbara. "Black Art." Art in America, Vol. 58,
     September/October, 1970, pp. 54-67.

     The author feels that Black artists face the same fate
     that White artists faced in the 1930s: lack of funds
     and patronage, lack of exposure and criticism, lack
     of opportunity to practice techniques and to experi-
     ence the quality of masterpieces. The photographs
     shown by the author shows the great range of work by
     Black artists in paintings, sculpture, architecture,
     graphics, and photography. The works of twenty-five
     artists are shown.

4
GENERAL ARTICLES

109. "Atlanta University Art Awards." <u>Jet</u>, Vol. 19, April 20, 1961, p. 51.

Lists winners in the Twentieth Atlanta University Exhibition of Black artists. A picture is shown of a patron looking at one the sculpture pieces.

110. "Afro-American Art: 1800-1950: <u>Ebony</u>, Vol. 23, February, 1968, pp. 116-118, 120-1<u>22</u>.

The City University of New York in cooperation with the Harlem Cultural Council and the New York Urban League sponsored an exhibit on "The Evolution of Afro-American Artists, 1800-1950."

111. "Afro-American Slide Program" <u>Art Journal</u>, Vol. 1, Fall, 1970, p. 85.

In a letter to the editor, Janice Ross of Alabama, wrote expressing doubt that the Kress Foundation had given the University of Southern Alabama $28,000 for a slide program on Afro-American art.

112. Akston, Joseph J. "Editorial." <u>Arts Magazine</u>, Vol. 45, May, 1971, p. 5.

The author cites the Metropolitan Musem attempt in 1968 to do an exhibit on Black arts as being a failure.

113. Allen, Cleveland G. "Our Young Artists." <u>Opportunity</u>, Vol. 1, June, 1923, pp. 24-25.

The author comments on the accomplishments of two Black artists, Albert A. Smith and Augusta Savage.

114. Allison, Madeline G. "Harleston! Who is E. A. Harleston?" <u>Opportunity</u>, Vol. 2, January, 1924, pp. 21-22.

(Allison, Madeline, G.)

The works of E. A. Harleston were on display at the
135th Street Library Exhibit of Paintings by Negro
Artists. His pictures were all on Negro subjects.
A short biographical sketch is given and two of his
paintings are displayed.

115.   Alloway, Lawrence. "Art." Nation, Vol. 212, May 10,
        1971.

The author notes the difficulty of art critics to
assess Black art. He cites the protest generated by
the Whitney Museum's Contemporary Black Artists in
America when Black artists withdrew their works because they had not been more responsibly involved.
Only six artists' works were shown. Alloway concludes that Black artists are haunted by racial ob-
ligations.

116.   "Along the Color Line." Crisis, Vol. 34, November,
        1927, p. 304.

Short paragraph on Hale Woodruff who had left for
Europe to study art in France, Italy, and Spain. The
trip was sponsored by the Harmon Foundation.

117.   "Along the Color Line." Crisis, Vol. 38, April, 1933,
        p. 128.

List of some winners of the Harmon Award in Fine Arts.
The winning art pieces are shown at the Art Center in
New York.

118.   "Along the Color Line - Middle South." Crisis, Vol.
        38, December, 1931, p. 428.

After studying four years in France, Hale Woodruff
joined the faculty of Atlanta University as Head of
the Art Department. He was born in Illinois, studied
in Indianapolis and attended the Chicago Art Institute.

119.   "Along the Color Line - Music and Art." Crisis, Vol.
        34, June, 1927, p. 124.

A portrait of Elijah Johnson and his two children
done by William E. Scott was exhibited at the Speed
Memorial Art Gallery in Louisville, Kentucky. He
also did a portrait of Mrs. W. R. Chavis and a character picture for the Marshall Field Art Gallery.

120.   "Along the Color Line - South East." Crisis, Vol.
        38, November, 1931, p.

Wilbert Warren held an exhibit of his paintings at
Spelman College. It contained twenty-eight colors,

three oils, and a number of drawings. A portrait of
W. E. B. DuBois received the greatest acclaim.

121. "Along the Color Line - The Middle States." _Crisis_,
Vol. 36, February, 1929, pp. 53-54.

The Harmon Awards were announced. In Fine Arts, Ar-
chibald Motley won the Gold Medal for his "Octoroon
Girls" (pictured) and May Howard Jackson won the
Bronze Medal for her bust of Kelly Miller. The Second
Annual Art Exhibit by the Harmon Fund was held with
Malvin G. Johnson winning first prize for "Swing Low
Sweet Chariot" (Pictured). J. W. Hardwick and Rich-
mond Barthe received honorary mentions.

122. "Amateur Artist." _Ebony_, Vol. 5, March, 1950, pp. 44-
46.

Prominent celebrities showed their artistic talents at
the annual Urban League Show. There were one hundred
twenty-three paintings on display. After the exhibition, the works were auctioned off. The Black celebrities included Duke Ellington, Ezzard Charles, Lena
Horne, Josh White, Joe Louis, and Dizzy Gillespie.
A picture of each artist and his works are included
in this article.

123. "Amateur Big League." _Life_, Vol. 15, April 16, 1951,
pp. 71-77.

Of the eleven artists featured in this article, one was
a Black. Reed Sligh's painting of an old bridge in
Massachusetts won third prize for oils.

124. "American Art or Negro Art?" _Nation_, Vol. 123, August
18, 1926, p. 151.

A letter to the editor written by Langston Hughes com-
menting on an article by George Schuyler criticizing
his statement that the Negro masses were the same as
White masses. Mr. Hughes felt that as long as the
Negro was a segregated race, he would reflect certain
racial and environmental differences. The true work
of art from the Negro artist is bound to reflect his
racial background, Mr. Hughes felt.

125. "American Negro Art." _Design_, Vol. 43, February, 1942,
pp. 27-28.

Exhibition of American Negro Art opened at the Down-
town Gallery in New York. Included seventy-five
paintings, sculpture, and prints produced by Nineteenth and Twentieth Century American Negro artists. The
aims of the exhibit were to show the value of Negro art
through its education programs and to set up a fund to
further develop Negro art by purchasing works of Negro

artists for exhibition.

126.   "American Negro Art." New Masses, Vol. 41, December
        30, 1941, p. 27.

        The Downtown Gallery in New York held an exhibit of
        seventy-five works by Black artists in the United
        States to raise money for the Negro Art Fund which
        would purchase art by living Black artists for pre-
        sentation to museums and to demonstrate their contri-
        butions to our culture.

127.   "American Negroes As Artists." Survey, Vol. 60,
        September 1, 1928, pp. 548-549.

        At the International House in New York, an exhibit
        sponsored by the Harmon Foundation was on display.
        Some disappointments were expressed that the exhibit
        gave no more of the special experiences and psycho-
        logy of the Negro. Three of the works are shown.

128.   "American Struggle: Three Paintings by Jacob Law-
        rence." Vogue, Vol. 130, July, 1957, pp. 66-67.

        Jacob Lawrence has produced sixty temperas (three are
        shown) in his series of American people from the War
        of Independence to the Industrial Revolution. A lover
        of history, Mr. Lawrence paints as he researches.
        The paintings in his series are soundly constructed
        with an economy of line and an extravagance of color.

129.   "An Art Exhibit Against Lynching." Crisis, Vol. 42,
        April, 1935, p. 106.

        The Arthur A. Newton Galleries in New York display,
        "An Art Commentary on Lynching," which was organized
        by the NAACP was a huge success. The Jacques Selig-
        mann Galleries was originally scheduled to do the ex-
        hibit but social and political pressures forced it to
        cancel. The exhibit consisted of oils, blacks and
        whites, wood carvings, and sculpture. The New York
        World Telegraph wrote "It is an exhibition which tears
        the heart and chills the blood." A wood carving and
        a painting from the exhibition are shown in the arti-
        cle.

130.   "An Artist Challenges the Bible." Sepia, Vol. 19,
        March, 1970, pp. 42-45.

        Floyd Sapp spends his time painting the history of the
        Black past. He credits Louis Michaux, owner of the
        National Memorial African Book Store, with bringing
        self pride and cultural enlightenment to the people of
        Harlem. Many of Sapp's paintings are of religious
        scenes in which he corrects the misrepresentation of
        Blacks in history. Eight of his religious paintings

are shown.

131.   "And the Migrants Keep Coming: A Negro Artist Paints
        the Story of the Great American Minority." Fortune,
        Vol. 24, November, 1941, pp. 102-109.

        Twenty-six works of artist Jacob Lawrence depict the
        great South-to-North migration of Negroes during the
        First World War. Some background is given on the life
        of Negroes in the South and why they were fleeing
        North. The paintings show the lynchings, police bru-
        tality, criminal injustices, lack of education, and em-
        ployment of the South, and then shows the poor housing,
        race riots, high death rates, freedom to vote, em-
        ployment for women, and a general better living condi-
        tion in the North. A picture of Mr. Lawrence is shown.

132.   "Another Artist." Crisis, Vol. 8, June, 1914, p. 66.

        B. E. Fountaine was given recognition as a promising
        artist by two art critics. He was at first a cabinet
        maker, then a waiter, but his talent was finally dis-
        covered at the Chicago World's Fair and he then be-
        came a janitor at Vincent O'Brien's Art Gallery where
        he developed his talent.

133.   "Archibald J. Motley, Jr." Opportunity, Vol. 6,
        April, 1928, pp. 114-115.

        Mr. Motley became the first Black artist to have a
        one-man show in a New York gallery when his works
        were put on display at the New Gallery. Mr. Motley's
        reputation rests on his portrayals of Black night life
        and his paintings on voodoo depicting the supersti-
        tions, dreams, and charms of the people of East Afri-
        ca. Three of his paintings are shown.

134.   "Art." Crisis, Vol. 1, January, 1911, p. 8.

        William E. Scott returned from Paris where he had
        lived for two years. A product of the Chicago Art
        Institute, Mr. Scott was a mural artist. He had some
        works exhibited in Paris and traveled over England,
        Holland, and Belgium.

135.   "Art." Crisis, Vol. 1, February, 1911, p. 10.

        William E. Scott had several paintings on exhibit at
        the Society of Western Artists. Henry O. Tanner had
        two paintings on exhibit at the Corcoran Gallery of
        Art in Washington, DC.

136.   "Art." Opportunity, Vol. 11, October, 1933, p. 316.

        The Harlem Adult Education Committee held an exhibit
        of works of forty-nine Negro artists. Paintings,

prints, drawings, and modeling were included. The
charcoals and lithographs were especially impressive.
The finest single piece was by Georgette Seabrook.

137.   "Art." Opportunity, Vol. 14, January, 1936, p. 32.

Speaking on an exhibition by Hale Woodruff, Ralph Mc-
Gill of the Atlanta Constitution wrote, "he does magnificent things with color, his yellows, and greens
being reminiscent even of the amazing color works
which made Vincent Van Gough so famous. They (his
paintings) have depth and something beyond the surface
of the oils."

138.   "Art." Opportunity, Vol. 14, July, 1936, pp. 219-220.

Notes that Ms. Augusta Savage was named as Assistant
Supervisor of the Federal Art Project of the WPA.
The Harlem Festival, part of the Federal Art Project,
had over 20,000 visitors to its exhibition on Black
art. Some judges included E. Simms Campbell, Wallace
Morgan, Aaron Douglas, and Russell Patterson. A picture of Ms. Savage is included.

139.   "Art at the University." Howard University Bulletin,
Vol. 35, March 15, 1957, p. 16.

The addition of the Alain Locke Collection of African
Negro sculpture and handicrafts increased the permanent holdings of Howard University Art Gallery to some
one thousand pieces. A brief elaboration of the founding of the Art Gallery, some of the persons responsi-
ble for its growth, the success of graduates, the
series of courses, and lectures, and the various collections are discussed.

140.   "Art By Negroes." Art Digest, Vol. 16, October 15,
1941, pp. 11-23.

One of the first exhibitions of Negro art was scheduled
by McMillen, Inc. in New York. It contained contemporary and African art. One picture, "Young Mother," by
Ernest Crithlow is shown.

141.   "Art Education for Negroes." Design, Vol. 46, December, 1944, p. 31.

Notes the contributions of Negro colleges in the South
in developing the variety, scope, and understanding of
the arts as a social force. Among the persons named
were James A. Porter and Alain Locke of Howard University and Hale Woodruff of the Atlanta University and
the Atlanta University Exhibition of Negro Painting.
Other schools mentioned were Dillard University, Stowe
Teachers College, Tillotson College, and Prairie View
College. Pottery from the students at Alabama College

was shown.

142. "Art Fellowship." Opportunity, Vol. 5, November,
      1927, p. 321.

      The Barnes Foundation admitted two Negro students to
      study art principles in its collection of modern and
      primitive art. The two students were Aaron Douglas
      and Gwendolyn Bennett. This short article notes the
      contributions of the foundation in interpretation of
      the various groups of Negro art expression.

143. "Art in Everyday Life at The Barnett-Aden Gallery."
      Women United, Vol. 9, October, 1949, pp. 16-17.

      The non-profit Barnett-Aden Gallery in Washington, DC
      aims to make the best contemporary art available to
      all people. Although the gallery is the creation and
      continual effort of Black artists and gives Black art-
      ists an opportunity to exhibit their works, member-
      ship is interracial.

144. "Art in Harlem." Art Front, Vol. 2, July/August,
      1936, p. 11.

      Dorrance Brooks Square in Harlem was turned into a gal-
      lery as an exhibition of works by Black artists and
      area residents, especially children, attending the
      WPA arts and crafts projects. The exhibit showed what
      could be done with children when given the proper
      training.

145. "Art Judge." Jet, Vol. 37, October 9, 1969, p. 27.

      Pictures of some of the judges and artists and their
      works at the Toledo, Ohio Black Artists' Show. The
      First National Bank and the Confederation of Black Art-
      ists co-sponsored the show.

146. "Art of Aaron Douglas." Crisis, Vol. 38, May, 1931,
      pp. 159-160.

      Mr. Douglas was commissioned to decorate Fisk Univer-
      sity's library. This article describes the mural that
      was done in three dimensions. The coloring was in pale
      tints with light from the central motif carried along
      in the contours of the figures. The general theme de-
      picts the importance of Negro history and various sym-
      bols and phases of education, depicting music, philo-
      sophy, science, literature, and drama are used. Mr.
      Douglas also decorated the Sherman Hotel in Chicago
      which consisted of a series of panelings of canvas de-
      picting the evolution of Negro dance.

147. "Art of Elizabeth Catlett." Contact, Vol. 5, Fall,
      1974, pp. 35-38.

Ms. Catlett has been winning prizes for her art work
since 1940 when she took first prize for her sculpture
at the American Negro Exposition. Her prized sculptures are done in terra cotta, brown marble, cedar,
walnut, stone, and bronze. A brief biographical sketch
of Ms. Catlett is included and a picture of Ms. Catlett
and two of her works are shown.

148. "Art of Henry O. Tanner." Ebony, Vol. 24, October,
      1969, pp. 60-62, 64-65.

      Some thirty-two years after Henry O. Tanner's death, the
      Frederick Douglass Institute and National Collection of
      Fine Arts in Washington, DC gave a retrospective exhi-
      bition of his works. Included were eighty paintings,
      drawings, and studies by Mr. Tanner who left the
      United States in 1891 to live and paint in France. A
      biographical sketch is given and an analysis of some of
      his works. Notes that today his reputation rests on
      his religious works. His brilliant use of light to
      symbolize the presence of God, his subtle contrast of
      light and darkness and his unique combination of mystic-
      ism and realism constituted a personal wisdom of popu-
      lar appeal.

149. "Art of the Negro." Art News, Vol. 42, March 1-4,
      1943, p. 6.

      The Grand Rapids Art Galleries Art Exhibit on Negro
      Art attempted to show the past, present, and future of
      the Negro race by displaying one hundred paintings.
      It showed African art from the Congo, Ivory Coast, Su-
      dan, etc. plus dramatic and colorful modern adult
      paintings and childrens' pictures from Negro children
      in the area schools.

150. "Artists Portray a Black Christ." Ebony, Vol. 26,
      April, 1971, pp. 176-178, 180.

      The growing trend toward a Black theology and as more
      Black people accept the premise that God was Black,
      the more artists will turn to Christ as a subject for
      meaningful paintings. Black artist, Alvin Hollings-
      worth, used his Black Prophet as a "philosophical sym-
      bol" of any of the modern prophets who have been try-
      ing to show us the right way. To him, Malcolm X and
      Martin Luther King, Jr. were such prophets. Eight
      paintings depicting a Black Christ were shown.

151. Ashton, Dore. "African and Afro-American Art: The
      TransAtlantic Tradition at the Museum of Primitive Art."
      Studio, Vol. 176, pp. 202-203.

      To meet the demands of Black militants to have art of
      the third world represented, the Museum of Primitive
      Art opened its season with "African and Afro-American

(Ashton, Dore)

Art: The TransAtlantic Tradition." The Exhibit suggested a new interest in African studies. Much credit
was given to Professor Robert F. Thompson of Yale for
his contribution to tracing individual African artists.
Two of the art pieces are shown.

152. "Atlanta's Annual." Time, Vol. 45, April 9, 1945, p. 65.

The Fourth Annual Atlanta University Art Exhibit ex-
clusively for Negroes in the United States featured
eighty-two paintings by forty-eight artists. Some canvasses were flavored with expressionism and romanticism
but most had a primitive quality. Four of the exhibition paintings are included.

153. Avery, Verna. "By Her Own Bootstraps." Opportunity,
Vol. 22, January/March, 1944, pp. 17, 42.

Ms. Beulah Woodward, a unique artist because she put
her knowledge to use in the field of ethnology. Her
realistic African masks were the result of years of
painstaking research. She studied ancient and modern
methods of mask making; she discovered a reason for
every detail in the masks. She made masks to preserve
the details of various Negroid types for future study.

154. _____. "Sargent Johnson." Opportunity, Vol. 17,
July, 1939, pp. 213-214.

Primarily interested in racial expression, Mr. Johnson
worked in many different mediums: wood, marble, terra
cotta, beaten copper, clay, plastic, terrazzo, and
others. The most striking of his works was a series of
copper masks. His most popular figure was a small
terra cotta head, "Chester," which won an award in
1931. This is shown in the article. Mr. Johnson has
won many awards including the Harmon Award.

155. Baker, James H., Jr. "Art Comes to the People of Harlem," Crisis, Vol. 46, March, 1939, pp. 78-80.

The Harlem Community Art Center, which opened December
20, 1937, served the Harlem community not only as a
teaching facility for specific interest groups and lectures, but went to any club or organization interested
in art. The center offered special assistance to the
community's artists. The center's history is traced
back to the 1920s when works were being shown at the
135th Street Branch of the New York Public Library.
This illuminating and historical story on the Center has
given rise to other centers throughout the Southeast
and notes the contributions by the people and some or-
ganizations in helping young artists.

156.   Balch, Jack.   "Democracy at Work: The People's Art
        Service Center in St. Louis." Magazine of Art, Vol.
        36, February, 1943, pp. 66-68.

        As part of the WPA art program, the People's Art Ser-
        vice Center opened under the sponsorship of local art-
        ists, art organizations, and laymen. The aim of the
        center was to give Negroes a more equal educational
        experience in art. The center opened with an exhibit
        by E. Simms Campbell. It was open to children and
        adults and offered courses in advertising, design,
        clay modeling, life and portrait drawing, dress de-
        signing, painting, and weaving.

157.   Barnes, Albert C. "Negro Art and America." Survey,
        Vol. 53, March, 1925, pp. 668-669.

        In both ancient and modern Negro art, there is a faith-
        ful expression of a people and of an epoch in the
        world's evolution. The art of the Negro embodies his
        individual traits and reflects his suffering, aspira-
        tions, and joys over a longer period of oppression.

158.   "Bearden Paints 'The Iliad'." Art Digest, Vol. 23,
        November 15, 1948, pp. 32-33.

        The Niveau Gallery was showing the works of Romare
        Bearden. It consisted of water colors entitled "Ili-
        ad-Sixteen Variations" using the Homeric poems as an
        inspiration and as the central theme. "The Wall of
        Troy," which is shown is one of the more successful
        of the group with its brilliant composition and lucid-
        ity of color.

159.   Bearden, Romare. "A Master Looks Back." Black En-
        terprise, Vol. 6, December, 1975, pp. 64-65, 69.

        Looks at the progress Black artists have made since
        the Nineteenth Century and lists some of the famous
        and infamous Black artists and their achievements. A
        picture of Mr. Bearden is shown along with the works
        of three artists.

160.   _____. "The Negro Artist and Modern Art." Opportun-
        ity, Vol. 12, December, 1934, pp. 371-372.

        Mr. Bearden felt that foundations which help the
        Negro artist really hinder him. He made reference to
        the Harmon Foundation which he felt that in choosing
        the works of Negro artists allowed the Negro to ac-
        cept artificial and corrupt standards. Other factors
        which he felt hindered the development of the Negro
        artist was no valid standard of criticism, plus the
        Negro artist had no ideology or social philosophy.

161. "Beauford Delaney Retrospective." First World, Vol.
      2, Spring, 1978, p. 44.

      An exhibition entitled, "Beauford Delaney: A Retro-
      spectible," opened in April at the Studio Museum in
      Harlem and would run through July 2. A catalogue of
      his works done in France and the United States was
      also published. One painting, "Yaddio" is shown.

162. Bement, Alon. "Some Notes on a Harlem Art Exhibit."
      Opportunity, Vol. 11, November, 1933, pp. 340-341.

      The exhibit at the 135th Street Branch of the New York
      Public Library showed the creative efforts of children
      in the Harlem Art Workshop. Pictures of the children
      at work and some of their creations are shown. This
      insightful article showed that these children could
      create beauty in art without being formally trained
      in the area.

163. Bennett, Gwendolyn. "The Harlem Artists Guild." Art
      Front, Vol. 3, May, 1937, p. 20.

      Organized to guard the cultural, social, and economic
      integrity of Black artists, the Harlem Artists Guild
      expanded to include all artists. The Guild stood
      with artists and organizations to fight a united
      front for the freedom of all artists. Lecture, sym-
      posiums, debates, and exhibits were means by which the
      Guild wanted to create a cultural program to place
      the Black artist in a position of importance.

164. Bennett, Mary. "The Harmon Awards." Opportunity,
      Vol. 7, February, 1929, pp. 47-48.

      Brief history of the Harmon Awards and areas in which
      the awards are offered. Mrs. May Howard Jackson
      received the Bronze Award in Fine Arts for her sculp-
      ture piece. Ninety-one pieces of art were submitted
      and an exhibit was sponsored. A special $250 prize
      was given to Malvin Gray Johnson for his painting,
      "Swing Low Sweet Chariot."

165. Bentley, Florence Lewis. "William A. Harper." Voice
      of The Negro, Vol. 3, February, 1906, pp. 118-122.

      The annual Society of Western Artists exhibition held
      at the Chicago Institute. One canvas receiving great
      attention was the landscape, "Young Poplars and Wil-
      lows," by William A. Harper. This was his second
      exhibition with his first selling six of his nine can-
      vasses. Mr. Harper was becoming an artist who believed
      in the portrayal of the rich beauty of the American
      landscape. Critics noted that Mr. Harper's works show
      a dignity and strength which inspires a renewed rever-
      ence for nature. A brief biographical sketch is in-

(Bentley, Florence Lewis)

cluded and four of his paintings are shown. A picture of Mr. Harper is included in this book.

166.   Berenson, Ruth. "A Different American Scene." National Review, Vol. 26, August 16, 1974, pp. 930-931.

Notes the Whitney Museum's closing season exhibition
of the full length retrospective works of Jacob Lawrence. Most of his best works dating from the 1930s
to the 1940s celebrate the little known heroes of
Black History. His prewar works were somewhat primitive and he has been accused of Uncle Tomism for his
espousal of integration in pictures.

167.   "Biggest Art Show." Ebony, Vol. 1, August, 1946,
pp. 46-49.

The Annual Atlanta University Art Show presented the
works of the best Negro artists in the country. The
fifth show had $1,400 in prizes, with items by forty-
six artists. The show began in 1942 by Hale Woodruff.
It was the only United States art exhibition exclu-
sively for Negro artists. Nine pictures of various
artists and their works are shown.

168.   "Black Art: What Is It?" The Art Gallery, April,
1970, pp. 32-35.

The editors of Art Gallery invited both Black and
White artists to give their view on Black art. White
response was scarce. Such Black artists as Romare
Bearden, Lois Mailou Jones, Malcolm Bailey, Faith
Ringgold, and Jan van der Mack responded.

169.   "Black Artist." Arts Magazine, Vol. 41, Summer, 1967,
p. 6.

Raymond Saunders wrote a letter in criticism of the
article in the May issue of Arts Magazine by Ishmael
Reed. He feels that Mr. Reed's documentation of Black
art was sparse. On one hand, Mr. Reed supports the
cause of Black artists; on the other hand, lumps all
artists into one bag.

170.   "Black Artists of the 1930s, Studio Museum in Harlem."
Artforum, Vol. 7, February, 1969, pp. 65-67.

An exhibit, "Invisible Americans," Black artists of
the 1930s, held in Harlem received wide acclaim because at the same time the Whitney Museum was also sur-
veying art in the 1930s but neglected to include many
Black artists. There were many protests against the
Whitney Museum. A critical analysis is given of the
Invisible Americans exhibit with the most criticism

being that it was done in haste and with lack of attention to historical perspective. Most notable was
the failure to include a Black style of the 1920s and
1930s known as "le style nègre."

171. "Black Artists: Two Generations." <u>School Arts</u>, Vol.
       71, December, 1971, pp. 21-28.

       This exhibition held at Newark Museum in 1971 shows a
       combination of the museums pioneering Black artists
       with works of twenty-two artists of the 1930s and
       1940s and that of thirty-four contemporary artists.
       Both generations show great diversity in style and
       subject matter. Ten works by various artists are
       shown.

172. "Black Image/Black Art." <u>Phase II</u>, Vol. 1, Spring,
       1971, pp. 31-32.

       An exhibit presented by the Northern California Medi-
       cal, Dental, Pharmaceutical Wives Auxillary was given
       as part of a concern of Northern California residents
       for better health, mind, and spirit. The artist can
       help portray a healthy self image which also promotes
       better health.

173. "Black Madonnas." <u>Ebony</u>, Vol. 15, December, 1959,
       pp. 140-142, 146, 148.

       Notes the many White artists who have sculptured and
       painted the Virgin Mary as a Black Madonna. Some of
       these artistic works go back centuries. At least
       four countries and hundreds of European, Central,
       and South American cities have shrines to Black Ma-
       donas. It explains the legends of these shrines from
       various countries, the miracles attributed to them,
       and the worship accorded these shrines. Sixteen pic-
       tures included the actual shrines, plus people in
       various countries worshipping the shrines.

174. "The Black Man's Gallery." <u>Urban West</u>, Vol. 1, Novem-
       ber/December, 1967, p. 10.

       The Black Man's Gallery opened in San Francisco's
       Fillmore ghetto devoted exclusively to the showing of
       of works by Black artists. Founder and sponsor, W. O.
       Thomas, Jr., felt that the artists brought a fresh vi-
       tality and sensitivity to their art. For some Blacks
       in the area it was the first works of Black artists
       they had ever seen.

175. Bloom, Janet. "5 + 1." <u>Arts Magazine</u>, Vol. 44,
       December, 1969/January, 1970, p. 56.

       This art show was developed by Frank Boweling for the
       State University of New York Art Gallery. The gallery

was divided by a barbed wire shirr of air whose bottom
scallops were of heavy chain. Several artists had
works in the exhibit including William Williams, Jack
Whitten, and Al Loving.

176.   Brady, Mary Beattie. "An Experiment in Inductive Service." Opportunity, Vol. 9, May, 1931, pp. 142-144.

Discusses the Harmon Foundation Awards which are given
out in nine different areas. In the area of art, Mr.
Harry Edmunds had the art exhibits held at the International House in New York and the latest which was re-
garded as outstanding in merit. The quality of the art
improved and the clientele increased.

177.   "Bright Sorrow." Time, Vol. 77, February 24, 1961,
pp. 60-63.

Fifty-eight of Jacob Lawrence's paintings went on exhibit at Allegheny College in Meadville, Pennsylvania.
This was the third stop in a nationwide tour of his
works arranged by the American Federation of Arts.
His works have a bright palette but still active a
sorrowful mood. His blues, greens, reds, yellows vie
for attention but never clash. Tension mounts in his
paintings but the threatened disorder never occurs.
Three of his paintings are shown, plus a picture of
Mr. Lawrence at work.

178.   Brooks, Mabel. "The Autobiography of an Artist."
Crisis, Vol. 39, February, 1932, p. 48.

Autobiographical sketch of Ms. Brooks on her early
life, education, entrance into art school, her teaching career as art teacher in Florida and Georgia. She
secured exhibits at Atlanta University for her students. She did an exhibit in 1925, afterward she
studied mural painting. She then went to Yale and
upon graduation went to Italy where she wrote this
article.

179.   Brown, Evelyn S. "The Harmon Awards." Opportunity,
Vol. 11, March, 1933, pp. 78-79.

History and growth of the Harmon Foundation Awards for
distinguished achievement by Blacks. The first pain-
ing in the area of art was so good that requests were
made to use them in exhibits across the country for
Negro History Week programs. This discerning article
showed the foresight of the founder, William E. Harmon, in recognizing the value of Black artists.

180.   Bundic, Dan. "People - Barbara Chase Ribound." Essence, Vol. 1, June, 1970, pp. 62-63, 71.

Interviews Ms. Chase-Ribound on her opinion on the

(Bundic, Dan)

role and responsibility of the Black artist vis-a-vis
the Black struggle, the kind of reception she received from the art establishment in Paris, opportunities for Black artists, and how Black artists can
maintain their individual Black identity. A picture
of Ms. Chase-Ribound in front of one of her works is
shown.

181   Bunin, Norman. "Andrew Wyeth: Painting the Invisible." Encore, Vol. 3, August, 1974, pp. 40-42.

Mr. Wyeth has used Blacks as models in some of his
most successful works. His realistic paintings of the
rural people and places in Maine and Pennsylvania are
well known. He had many Black friends and the one he
has painted most often is Willard Snowden, a merchant
seaman. Wyeth noted that Black people "have so much
imagination and such dignity."

182.   Butler, Joseph T. "The American Way with Art." Con-
noisseur, Vol. 176, March, 1971, pp. 206-212.

In this article on artists and art exhibits, one Black
artist is given attention. The art of Henry O. Tanner
which was on exhibit throughout the United States was
organized by the Frederick Douglass Institute in
Washington, DC. A short biographical sketch of Tanner
is given and at the final stop of the exhibition at
the Philadelphia Museum of Art, it was announced that
one of Tanner's paintings had been discovered in the
basement of a school for the deaf. Four of Tanner's
paintings are included in this article.

183.   "CAA and Negro Colleges." Art Journal, Vol. 17,
Winter, 1969, p. 228.

Letters written by Edward Wilson, Chairman of the Art
Department at New York State University in Binghampton
and James A. Porter, Head of the Art Department at
Howard University stress the need for the College Art
Association to promote art programs in Negro schools.
Wilson felt that the CAA should organize a symposium
on art for Negro college presidents to make them aware
of the value of art. Porter suggested a long term program to help trace the inadequacies of art education
in Negro colleges.

184.   Caldwell, Bill. "Romare Bearden: Art is the Soul of
People." Encore, Vol. 1, October, 1972, pp. 58-61.

Mr. Bearden is noted as a mathematician, poet, philosopher, historian, and writer, is also one of the
world's most imaginative painters. His use of collage records the Black past and present. Mr. Bearden

(Caldwell, Bill)

cites such artists as Claude McKay, Jacob Lawrence, and others to have their works recognized.

185.   _____. "Romare Bearden." Essence, Vol. 6, May, 1975, pp. 70-73.

Notes that his exhibition at the Cordier & Ekstrom Gallery was sold out in two weeks. In stating why he used the collage, Mr. Bearden said that when some detail such as an eye or hand is taken out of its original context and placed in a different space, it acquires a different quality. Most of his subject matter deals with urban and Southern rural Black life and some themes from the Islands. A picture of Mr. Bearden and two of his works are shown.

186.   Campbell, Mary Schmidt. "Critical and Cynical." Art News, Vol. 74, October, 1975, pp. 81-82.

The Herbert F. Johnson Museum at Cornell University was the last stop for the Benny Andrews Exhibit "Bicentennial Series." Four multi-panel mural sized collage paintings show the demoralizing morality and repressive social structures in America. Thirty-three drawings and twenty oils and oil-collages serve as travel guides. The four series are, "Symbols, 1971," "Trash, 1972," "Circle," and "Sexism, 1974."

187.   Canady, John. "America's First Major Black Artist." Carnegie Magazine, Vol. 44, April, 1970, pp. 138-139.

Notes an exhibit by Henry O. Tanner at the Carnegie Institute. Organized by the Frederick Douglass Institute of Negro Arts and History, it was first shown at the Smithsonian Institution and will travel to other art museums. Born in 1859, Mr. Tanner died in Paris in 1937 where he lived and worked. He was married to a White woman and they had one son. Mr. Tanner's works received awards in international exhibits. Two of his paintings are shown.

188.   _____. "The Art of Romare Bearden." Contact, Vol. 5, Spring, 1974, pp. 32-39.

Although this is a book review of Mr. Bearden's, The Art of Romare Bearden, the author gives an indepth analysis of Bearden and his works. Notes Bearden's concern with the problems of all Black artists and has given his support by becoming director of the Cinque Gallery, which displayed works of minority artists and later director of the Harlem Cultural Council. A picture of Mr. Bearden and six of his works are shown.

189.   "Careers in Color Line." Ebony, Vol. 1, December,
        1945, pp. 46-50.

        The past traditions of Black artists to imitate the
        White man's paintings are now past. The Black artist
        can now make a living out of conquering color---both
        on canvas and in the American mind. Notes the accom-
        plishments of Jacob Lawrence, Richmond Barthe, Horace
        Pippin, and Ellis Wilson who are pictured at work.
        There are four other paintings by various Black art-
        ists included.

190.   "Carole Byard: An Artist's Lifestyle." Black Enter-
        prise, Vol. 6, December, 1975, pp. 29-30, 132.

        Ms. Byard's work often relates to various dimensions
        of the human experience. It shows several pictures of
        Ms. Byard at work.

191.   Carter, Elmer A. "E. Simms Campbell - Caricaturist."
        Opportunity, Vol. 10, March, 1932, pp. 82-85.

        An account of how Mr. Campbell came to New York to do
        magazine illustrations for Opportunity and other maga-
        zines. After leaving St. Louis, Mr. Campbell entered
        the Academy of Design in New York. It notes the part
        Ed Graham played in his career. Mr. Graham introduced
        Campbell to various magazine editors and showed them
        his work. Within a year he was doing illustrations
        for several magazines. A picture of Mr. Campbell plus
        three of his magazine illustrations are shown.

192.   "Cartoonist for Playboy: Esquire Dies at Age 65."
        Jet, Vol. 39, February 18, 1971, pp. 12-13.

        E. Simms Campbell dies at the White Plains, New York
        Hospital. Although highly successful as a cartoonist,
        few knew he was Black. He had graduated from Chicago
        Art Institute and did freelance work for such maga-
        zines as Colliers, Life, Playboy, Esquire, and Satur-
        day Evening Post. He later moved to Switzerland and
        stayed for fourteen years. He has won many awards
        for his cartoons.

193.   Casey, Bernie. "Why I Paint." The Art Gallery,
        April, 1970, pp. 30-31.

        Mr. Casey, a former football player, turned poet and
        actor, chose to paint because it was a necessary part
        of his being. He feels that Black artists must real-
        ize that they have an aesthetic feeling and must paint
        and not wait for acceptance, for validation of their
        existence, and understand that the most important
        thing is to be true to his art.

194.   "Ceramics by Tony Hill." Ebony, Vol. 2, November,
        1946, pp. 31-35.

        Tony Hill's earthenware has sold in almost every large
        city in America and in six countries abroad. His
        modern ceramics are functional. He never repeats his
        colors and makes pieces in colors selected by his
        customers. A short biographical sketch is included
        and seven pieces are shown plus pictures of he and his
        staff at work.

195.   "Charles White." Artforum, Vol. 2, April, 1964, p. 49.

        His exhibit at Heritage Gallery was a hit in the field
        of commercial exhibitions. The exhibit consisted of
        lino-cuts and Chinese ink stick drawings. His works
        are a little sentimental and he can be labeled as an
        incurable romantic. One ink drawing, "Birmingham
        Totem," is shown.

196.   "Charles White and Ernest Lacy." Artforum, Vol. 4,
        October, 1965, p. 15.

        Both artists had an exhibition at the Heritage Gallery.
        Both Southern Californian artists know the importance
        of knowing one's medium. They are both printmakers
        dealing in traditional imagery. Lacy's work seems to
        offer greater variety. One etching by Lacy, "Trio,"
        is shown.

197.   "Chinaware Decorator." Ebony, Vol. 3, September,
        1948, pp. 59-61.

        Seventy year old Mrs. Alma J. Scott has had seven
        exhibitions in Washington, DC of her china decorations
        and won high praise from collectors and critics. Her
        hand painted china was worth more than $20,000. She
        won a blue ribbon at the Cocoran Gallery of Art in
        Washington, DC for her work. Eight of her pieces in-
        cluding vases, tea sets, and lamps are shown plus
        pictures of her at work.

198.   "Church Muralist." Ebony, Vol. 7, June, 1952, pp. 66-
        68, 70.

        The murals of an untrained Black artist, Aaron Miller,
        dramatize in fourteen pictures the closing scenes of
        the Passion of Christ. They are painted on the walls
        of the Emanuel Church of God in Christ in San Fran-
        cisco with each being 14' high and 9' wide. Art cri-
        tics highly praised his work which was completed in
        fourteen months. Six pictures of the murals and Mr.
        Miller at work are shown.

199.   "Clarence Major Interviews: Jacob Lawrence, The Ex-
        pressionist." The Black Scholar, Vol. 9, November,

1977, pp. 14-27.

Mr. Major interviews Jacob Lawrence at Mr. Lawrence's studio at the University of Washington on January 10, 1977. They talked about Mr. Lawrence's works in gouache and tempera, about his artistic style, how critics view his works, his commitment to the struggle for justice, if his works are known in Europe, etc. four of his works are featured and a picture of Mr. Lawrence and Mr. Majors are shown.

200.   Clay, Jean. "The Implications of Negritude." _Studio International_, Vol. 172, July, 1966, pp. 51-53.

The First World Festival of Negro Arts held in Dakar included a colloquim, one hundred theater and dance productions, and many exhibits of classical and modern art. It did not discuss past African cultures, but talked about negritude and the future of Negro art.

201.   Coffin, Patricia. "Black Artists in a White Art World." _Look_, Vol. 33, January 7, 1969, pp. 66-69.

Article talks about the works of Daniel La Rue Johnson. His was the only work by a Black artist in the Whitney Museum. Notes that Mr. Johnson's dream is to channel the hostility of the ghetto youth into creativity.

202.   Cole, Helen. "Henry O. Tanner, Painter." _Brush and Pencil_, June, 1900, pp. 97-107.

A lengthy biographical sketch on Mr. Tanner and notes that although he was an excellent painter, he does not get that much publicity of his works. Eight of his works are shown, plus one of him in his studio, and a painting of him done by H. D. Murphy.

203.   "Connecticut High School Hosts Barnett-Aden Gallery." _Jet_, Vol. 53, January 26, 1978, p. 14.

Students and faculty members of Weaver High School in Hartford, Connecticut were hosts of the distinguished Barnett-Aden Art Collection. The collection consists of over seventy pieces of Afro-American art dating back to the Nineteenth Century to the present. The gallery opened in Washington, DC in 1943.

204.   "Contemporary Negro Art." _Arts Magazine_, Vol. 31, October, 1956, pp. 58-59.

A group of Black American artists are shown along with the work from the Romaine Destosses School at Elizabethville. Only one of the American artists' works is on Black art.

205.   Coombs, Orde. "Ausby Paints that Special Feeling."
        Encore, Vol. 1, September, 1972, pp. 56-57.

        Ellsworth Ausby went to the School of Visual Arts and
        has done a lot paintings dealing with the Black male.
        He notes the three periods of his work.

206.   _____. "Al Hollingsworth: Portrait of the
        Artist as a Believer." Essence, Vol. 1, February,
        1971, pp. 50-51, 70-71.

        Interview with Mr. Hollingsworth on his exhibit, "The
        Prophet: Series," at the Studio Museum in Harlem.
        He talks about his early struggles, and the break that
        NBC gave him to do a painting program which was put
        on prime time television.

207.   "Country Gentlemen." Ebony, Vol. 2, August, 1947,
        pp. 9-15.

        The country's most successful illustrator, E. Simms
        Campbell, values his secluded home life where he pro-
        duces his illustrations. He talks of the models he
        used for his "cuties" series, his gag cartoons, the
        discrimination against Blacks, how long it took him
        to get started and attain his present prominence.
        Thirteen pictures of him at work with his family and
        friends are shown.

208.   Craig, Randall J. "Focus on Black Artists: A Pro-
        ject for School and Communities." School Arts, Vol.
        70, November, 1970, pp. 30-33.

        "Afro-American Artists: 1800-1969" was presented as
        a vehicle for bringing the works of renown Black
        American artists, both past and contemporary, to the
        attention of the schools and the community. Two
        hundred forty-three works were in the traveling ex-
        hibit which was sponsored by several funds and groups.
        Looks briefly at the significance of African art on
        the art of today. Seven works by various artists are
        shown.

209.   "The Creative Art of Negroes." Opportunity, Vol. 1,
        August, 1923, p. 240-245.

        The Negro artists of this time seemed to express them-
        selves by following the pattern of African culture.
        He was often judged by his African culture and was ex-
        pected to reflect it in his work. Little attention
        has been given to the pure and uninfluenced art of
        Negroes. The rest of the article deals with an Afri-
        can Art Exhibit procurred by Stewart Culin of the
        Brooklyn Museum when he was in Europe in 1921-1922.
        He notes that all forms of American culture including
        textiles, sculpture, and metal works. Twelve examples

of African art are shown.

210.   "Chrichlow Ernest." ·Freedomways, Vol. 4, Summer,
        1964, p. 455.

        Mr. Chrichlow stated that his paintings were mostly
        about the urban Negro and poverty. He said he liked
        to accentuate the dignity and strength in the Negro
        character.

211.   "David Mosley: Soul Artist." Sepia, Vol. 19, March,
        1970, pp. 43-45.

        This artist who was born in Louisiana in 1941, has
        done paintings of many Black public figures like
        Martin Luther King, Jr., Stevie Wonder, Eldridge
        Cleaver, Jimi Hendrix, and others. His works became
        part of his new "Watts Culture" and many critics have
        seen the style of Rembrandt in his works. Three of
        his paintings are featured, plus a picture of Mr.
        Mosley seated among some of his paintings.

212.   Dawson, Charles C. "The Negro in Art." The Southern
        Workman, Vol. 58, January, 1929, pp. 12-13.

        Prior to 1927 there had been no single or group move-
        ments to exhibit Black art. In November, 1927, "The
        Negro in Art Work" was the first exhibit of modern
        Negro artists as a group given by The Museum of Fine
        Arts. It was the first time materials by Negro art-
        ists had been on exhibit showing the real history of
        contemporary American Negro art. This article notes
        the great response of the public to the exhibit and
        to the stimulation of artists for proficient achieve-
        ment.

213.   "Dealers." Black Enterprise, Vol. 6, December, 1975,
        pp. 43-45.

        Notes the efforts of Black art dealers who help Black
        artists get their works displayed and sold. Looks at
        Linda Bryant of Just Above Mid-Town Gallery, Samella
        Lewis of The Gallery, and Larry Randall of Randall
        Galleries. Pictures of each dealer in their galleries
        are shown.

214.   "Detroit's Picasso." Our World, Vol. 7, January,
        1952, p. 58.

        A painter at a Chicago nightclub, Mr. Walter Sanford,
        studied at the Chicago Art Institute. Developing a
        love for expressionism, his works were sponsored by
        the Judner Agency in Detroit. That city named him
        their "Picasso" and a favorite son.

215. De Vore, Jesse. "Negro Art Theme Winning - Successful Brooklynite." Crisis, Vol. 70, April, 1963, pp.
228-230.

Freelance artist, Tom Feelings', career soared after
he did the illustrations for the NAACP's voter regis-
tration book entitled, "The Street Where You Live."
He went on to do illustrations for Look, Harper's,
and The Reporter. He has had one-man shows at the
J. Walter Thompson Advertising Agency, The Park Vil-
lage Gallery, Morgan State College, and Atlanta University. A picture of Mr. Feelings is included plus
two of his illustrations.

216. Dewey, John. "The Negroes' Contribution to Art."
Opportunity, Vol. 3, September, 1925, p. 280.

At the dedication of the Barnes Foundation, Mr. Dewey
noted the finest collection of African art. The
foundation served the cause of bringing all people of
the world together in harmony and showed the artistic
capability of the Negro to do beautiful and significant work.

217. "Dimensions of Black, La Tolla Museum." Artforum,
Vol. 8, May, 1970, pp. 83-84.

An exhibition of contemporary and historical Black
artists organized by Jehanne Teilhet and his students.
The first part of the exhibit is a visual survey of
African objects. The second part documents historic
Black art from America. The war period is scant although Jacob Lawrence is included. The last part is
devoted to the influence of Black art on White artists.

218. Douglas, Carlyle, C. "Romare Bearden." Ebony, Vol.
31, November, 1975, pp. 116-118, 120-122.

Recognized since the 1940s as one of America's leading
abstractionists, Mr. Bearden was influenced by E.
Simms Campbell and Charles Alston. He uses exaggerated
physical features to stress the function of those features and to evoke more extensions. By 1949, he had
exhibited at major galleries in Washington, DC, Paris,
and New York, and leading museums throughout the
country. His works sell for upwards to $20,000. In
explaining what is "extensions" he said that "everything must have more than one meaning so that nothing
becomes localized." Four of his paintings are shown
plus several of him at work, with his family and with
fellow artists.

219. Douglas, Emory. "Art in Service for the People." The
Black Scholar, Vol. 9, November, 1977, pp. 55-57.

(Douglas, Emory)

Mr. Douglas feels that Black artists should create
images that will stimulate awareness of the conditions
of racism, such as unemployment, poor health care, police brutality, lack of decent housing, etc.   Six
pictures by Mr. Douglas showing various examples of
racism are shown. Mr. Douglas is a university lec-
turer on art and presently is the artist for the
Black Panther Newspaper. He is a peoples' artist who
has exhibited in the United States, Africa, Asia, and
Latin America.

220.   "Drawings of Charles White: Images of Dignity." The
        Negro Digest, Vol. 16, June, 1967, pp. 40-41.

        Biographical sketch of Mr. Charles White whose works
        have been exhibited in many galleries. He has re-
        ceived the Rosenwald Foundation Award. He has done
        murals for the Chicago Public Library, Tuskegee In-
        stitute, and his most noteworthy one at Hampton Insti-
        tute. The article tells of a new book devoted to
        White in which ninety reproductions of his works from
        the time of his paintings are featured. Eight of his
        paintings are featured.

221.   Drummond, Dorothy. "Philadelphia." Art Digest, Vol.
        26, March 1, 1952, p. 12.

        The Twelfth Annual Invitational Exhibit was sponsored
        by the Pyramid Club, a leading Black social organiza-
        tion. One hundred fifteen paintings and sculptures
        with Charles H. Alston as guest artist, touched all
        phases of current art.

222.   _____. "Philadephia New." Art Digest, Vol. 24,
        March 1, 1950, p. 9.

        The Pyramid Club, Philadelphia's leading Black social
        club, was holding its Tenth Annual Exhibition of Paint-
        ings and Sculpture. The show had over one hundred
        paintings but few Black artists are shown and subject
        matter on Black life was completely abandoned. The
        show's aim was for better racial understanding and cul-
        tural sympathy.

223.   DuBois, W. E. B. "Criteria of Negro Art." Crisis,
        Vol. 32, October, 1926, pp. 290, 292, 294, 296-297.

        The address on art was delivered by Dr. DuBois at a
        conference of the NAACP. This address deals mostly
        with discrimination in the literary field, but talks
        briefly of Black artists and how they have to work on
        their own because art schools would not accept them.
        What Dr. DuBois was saying, in essence, was that the
        White public demands from its artists, both literary

(DuBois, W. E. B.)

and pictorial, racial judgments which deliberately
distort the views of the colored races.

224.   Dunbar, Rudolph. "The Influence of Negro Art." Cri-
        sis, Vol. 46, January, 1939, pp. 13-18.

Author stated that early Negro art has died out with
no effort being made to revive it or develop it from
where it left off. Modern interest in Negroes has
been an attempt to recapture the past without the
realization that the modern Negro lives in a modern
world. Mr. Dunbar felt that the Negro race should
realize the importance of its past cultures and dis-
cover the necessity of evolving a contemporary culture.

225.   Elliot, Jeffrey. "Charles White: Portrait of an
        Artist." The Negro History Bulletin, Vol. 41, May/
        June, 1978, pp. 825-828.

Mr. Elliot interviews Charles White on his artistic
talents, his character, and his concerns, and how his
art deals with the full gamut of human spirit. A
picture of Mr. White and two of his works are shown.

226.   _____. "Charles White: Portrait of an Artist."
        Sepia, Vol. 26, February, 1978, pp. 58-64.

Charles White's work is known for its power, drama,
and pathos. He sees strength and nobility in people.
He makes brilliant use of space, contrast, line, form,
and texture and his work has rhythm, motion, spirit-
uality, and serenity. Mr. Elliot asked Mr. White
why he decided to become an artist, if there are un-
told themes in his works, if he has seen a growth in
his artistic ability and personal development, the
special problems of Black artists, criticisms of his
works, and the role art plays as a liberating force.
Five of his paintings and several of the artist are
shown.

227.   Ellison, Ralph. "Romare Bearden: Paintings and Pro-
        jections." Crisis, Vol. 77, March, 1970, pp. 80-86.

A series of collages and projections by Romare Bearden
are shown. Notes that Bearden has blended strange
visual harmonies out of the shrill, indigenous dicho-
tomies of American life and in doing so, reflected the
irrepressible thrust of a people to endure and keep
its intimate sense of its own identity.

228.   Fabio, Sarah W. "Afro-American Art: A Historical Per
        spective." Phase II, Vol. 1, Summer, 1970, pp. 27-31.

(Fabio, Sarah W.)

Author feels that as in all other areas, the Black
artists have been repressed. Notes that Aaron Douglas,
Archibald Motley, and Hale Woodruff as some who have
been popular, especially during the Harlem Renaissance.
Names Jacob Lawrence, Romare Bearden, and Charles
White as artists who passed their tradition to the cur-
rent generation. Criticizes the New York Exhibit,
"Harlem on My Mind," which did not represent the Black
experience in America.

229.   Farrow, William McKnight. "The Chicago Art League."
        Crisis, Vol. 34, December, 1927, pp. 344-358.

        The Chicago Art League was formed as part of the YMCA
        to carry on lectures, demonstrations, exhibits, etc.
        They encouraged young people in the study of art and
        its motto of clean up and beautify to help enhance
        the run down neighborhoods in Chicago.

230.   Fauset, Jessie. "Henry Ossawa Tanner." Crisis, Vol.
        27, April, 1924, pp. 255-258.

        Ms. Fauset interviewed Henry O. Tanner who studied
        painting, drawing, and modeling at the Philadelphia
        Academy of Fine Arts. He went to Europe in 1892,
        which became his home. By 1897, he was exhibited at
        the Paris Salon and he was given the Legion of Honor.

231.   Fax, Elton C. "Four Rebels in Art." Freedomways,
        Vol. 4, Spring, 1964, pp. 215-225.

        This article appraises the works of Elizabeth Catlett,
        a sculptress, painter, and printermaker; Jacob Law-
        rence, the painter who depicted the Depression in
        Harlem; Charles White, who painted murals, made litho-
        graphs, and woodcuts; and John T. Biggers, whose
        paintings, drawings, and sculpture depicted the
        Negroes of the rural South. Mr. Fax captured the re-
        bellious nature of each artist and described how the
        circumstances of their early lives led them into art.

232.   Feelings, Tom. "Black Art." Black Collegian, Vol. 8,
        March/April, 1978, p. 40.

        Four paintings by Tom Feelings are shown: "Mother and
        Child," "Middle Passage (Slave Ship)," and "To Be A
        Slave," and "BedSty."

233.   "Festival Scrapbook." Negro Digest, Vol. 15, August,
        1966, pp. 85-90.

        Thirteen pictures of people, exhibits, and performances
        at the First World Festival of Negro Arts are shown.

234.   "Fifty-Seven Negro Artists Presented in Fifth Harmon
       Foundation Exhibit." Art Digest, Vol. 7, March 1,
       1933, p. 18.

       The Fifth Annual Exhibition of Negro Artists was
       sponsored by the Harmon Foundation Art Center in New
       York. Fifty-seven artists with one hundred seven art
       pieces were represented. Sargent Johnson won first
       prize. Other winners were Palmer Hayden, William E.
       Artis, James Lesesne Wells, and James Allen. The
       first prize painting, Defiant, by Mr. Johnson is shown.

235.   Fine, Elsa Honiz. "The Afro-American Artist: A
       Search for Identity." Art Journal, Vol. 29, Fall,
       1969, pp. 32-35.

       The search for identity by the Black artist has been
       a continuing process since the Nineteenth Century.
       Langston Hughes urged the Negro to portray their
       Blackness in their art. Looks briefly at the Negro
       in art up through the Twentieth Century. A short ac-
       count of Black art with a bibliography of sources.

236.   "First Generation of Artists." Survey Graphic, Vol.
       28, March, 1939, pp. 224-225.

       The Baltimore Museum of Art held the first exhibition
       of works by Black artists in that city. Paintings,
       prints, drawings, and sculpture by some thirty art-
       ists were assembled with the aid of the Harmon Founda-
       tion. Seven paintings by four artists (Elton Fax,
       Malvin Johnson, Archibald Motley, and Jacob Lawrence)
       are included.

237.   "First Negro National, Atlanta University." Magazine
       of Art, Vol. 35, May, 1942, p. 185.

       Atlanta University was the setting for the National
       Annual Art Exhibit by Black artists. The purpose of
       this show was to present the works of members of the
       Atlanta group and their peers in other centers.

238.   "First World Festival of Negro Arts." Negro Digest,
       Vol. 14, August, 1965, pp. 62-69.

       Article on the prospectus of the First World Festival
       of Negro Arts which was scheduled for Senegal during
       April, 1966. The theme was to show the motives and
       contrasts of Negro art. African art was to be shown
       plus an exhibit selected by participating states on
       contemporary sculpture, painting, gouache, engraving
       arts, illustrated books, and tapestries.

239.   "Four Portraits of Negro Women." Survey, Vol. 53,
       March, 1925, pp. 685-688.

Winold Reiss had drawn four portraits of Negro women:
a woman from the Virgin Islands, a librarian, two
school teachers, and one of Elsie Johnson McDougold.

240.   "Four Portraits: Richard Hunt." Saturday Review, Vol.
        58, November 15, 1975, p. 16.

        Hunt works in plastic arts. He has mastered the weld-
        ing torch and most of his works are abstracts. He had
        done many one-man shows, commissions, and extensive
        gallery and museum exhibitions. He has been criticized
        for ignoring his cultural heritage.

241.   "From the Harmon Foundation Art Exhibit, 1934." Op-
        portunity, Vol. 12, June, 1934, p. 186.

        Three pictures, one by Aaron Douglas, and two by
        Charles H. Alston were shown as part of the entries in
        the 1934 Harmon Foundation Exhibition.

242.   "Frontpiece." Opportunity, Vol. 8, February, 1930,
        p. 38.

        A picture of "The Banjo Player" painted by Hale A.
        Woodruff is shown. It had been submitted in the art
        section of the Harmon Awards.

243.   Fuller, Hoyt. "Festival Postscripts." Negro Digest,
        Vol. 15, June, 1966, pp. 82-87.

        Eight criticisms of the American Committee for the
        First World Festival of Negro Art. The complaint was
        against the selection of a White to head the committee
        and some of the entertainers selected for the festival.
        Also the fact that Blacks had little to do with the
        selection of entertainers and at times knew little of
        what activities were planned.

244.   Carver, Thomas H. "Dimensions of Black, La Jolla Mu-
        seum." Artforum, Vol. 9, May, 1970, pp. 83-84.

        An exhibit documenting the works of Black artists,
        both contemporary and historical periods and points of
        views. It was divided into four parts: African ob-
        jects; paintings and objects from the United States;
        a small section of art done between the world wars;
        and a section on the influence of Black art on White
        artists.

245.   Ghent, Henri. "And So It Is." School Arts, Vol. 68,
        April, 1969, pp. 21-26.

        Cites the new interest in Black art, with the redis-
        covery of the Nineteenth Century. Featured are Romare
        Bearden, Vivian Browne, Robert Still, and others. A
        picture of each artist and one work of each is shown.

246.   _____. "Quo Vadis Black Art." Art in America, Vol. 62, November/December, 1974, pp. 41-42.

Talks about the exhibit, "Directions in Afro-American Art," at Cornell University. It featured paintings, sculpture, and some graphic works by twenty-eight artists. Works of some of the renown Black artists were a special feature of the exhibit. There was a total of one hundred twenty-five works. Notes some of the outstanding artists in the exhibit. Mr. Ghent felt that the exhibit had such untimely content and had such deadening uniformity of style that it only numbed any potential political or esthetic impact.

247.   Glueck, Bruce. "Who's Minding the Easel?" Art in America, Vol. 56, January/February, 1968, pp. 112-113.

Notes an exhibit by Terry Dintenfass Gallery in New York. The exhibit deals with the life of Harriet Tubman. Art critic, Aline Saarinen, called Mr. Lawrence "a phenomenon almost unique in our time, a narrative painter." The mood of his paintings is that of compassion rather than protest. His rhythmically designed canvasses, done in tempera and casin, bear the stamp of an authoritative painter.

248.   Goodman, Michael Harris. "Joseph Clinton DeVillis: Seaman, Artist, Churchman." The Negro History Bulletin, Vol. 41, May/June, 1978, pp. 830-833.

Born June 17, 1878, little is known of DeVillis' early life. He enlisted in the Navy at sixteen and fought in the Battle of Manilla Bay for which he received a medal. After his discharge, he worked at the Rohlfs Art Gallery in New York. Landscapes and seascapes were his specialities. Most of his works are untitled and undated. He died at the young age of 33 in 1912.

249.   Graves, Earl G. "The Importance of Art Patronage." Black Enterprise, Vol. 6, December, 1975, pp. 5, 7.

Notes the problems that Black artists have in getting their works exhibited and notes that Black businessmen should encourage and support Black artists.

250.   Greene, Marjorie. "Fear and Art for an Ex-Wac." Opportunity, Vol. 25, Fall, 1947, pp. 200-201.

Benita Schuster joined the WACs and became a Signal Corps photographic artist on the post paper, propaganda artist with the Information and Education Service in the United States and the artist for her battalion overseas. She used oils, crayons, pen, and ink in her work and was admitted to the National Academy of Design solely on merit. She has a fear of failure but loses

(Greene, Marjorie)

this fear when she puts on canvas the things she feels.
Three pictures of Benita are shown plus one of her
paintings and one of her art reproductions are included.

251. Hagstrom, Frienda. "The Negro in the New Art Educa-
      tion." Design, Vol. 44, June, 1943, pp. 201-221.

      Lists the three trends in modern art education and how
      the Negro art student has contributed to it with his
      colorful and dramatic ability to portray and interpret
      his experiences. In this article Ms. Hagstrom shows
      the biased opinions of others who see the Negro as
      the happy and carefree being who releases his pent
      up emotions in dance, pantomime, and song. She feels
      this is also portrayed in his art by the use of bright
      colors, the unconscious use of rhythm.

252. Hall, Nick J. "Postman to Painter." Sepia, Vol. 20,
      December, 1971, pp. 72-74, 76, 78.

      This former postman moved to further his painting
      career. Edward Webster has had exhibits at the
      "Escuela de Nobles y Bellas," becoming the first North
      American artist to exhibit there. Critics felt that
      his works were his own personal interpretation of life.

253. "Harlem Adagio Dancer." Crisis, Vol. 39, July, 1932,
      p. 228.

      The work of Bradford Delaney was exhibited at the Art
      Gallery of the New York Public Library. The most
      noteworthy work was, "Harlem Adagio Dancer," which
      showed a special vitality.

254. "Harlem Artists' Guild." Art Front, Vol. 2, July/
      August, 1936, pp. 4-5.

      The Guild came out against the Harmon Foundation's
      efforts to collect the works of arts by Negroes to be
      shown at the Texas Centennial. The Guild felt that
      the Harmon Foundation was not a recognized art agency
      and could only look at art from a sociological stand-
      point. The Guild felt that the Foundation had too
      much influence over Negro art and arbiter of the Negro
      artists' fates through the philanthropic endeavors.

255. "Harlem Hospital Murals." Art Front, Vol. 2, April,
      1936, p. 3.

      Black artists employed in the Federal Arts Project
      were assigned to design murals for the Harlem Hospital.
      The works of four artists were rejected by the hospital
      superintendent as having too much Negro subject matter,

possible criticism of the Negro subject matter by the
Negro community and a feeling that his hospital should
not be singled out for treatment with Negro subjects.
The superintendent had already approved works by White
artists on White subject matter. The WPA planned to
fight for better conditions and freedom of expression
for Negro artists.

256.   "Harlem Types." Survey, Vol. 53, March, 1925, pp. 651-
654.

Winold Reiss presents a graphic interpretation of
Negro life. Although caricatures have pictured the
Negro as comical and grotesque, in real life, they are
more brooding and mystical. He shows a mother and
child, a woman lawyer, a boy scout, a college student,
and pictures of three young women.

257.   "Harmon Foundation Spreads Public Appreciation of Negro
Art." Art Digest, Vol. 9, June, 1935, p. 23.

For over a decade the Harmon Foundation had been carry-
ing on a program of teaching centers and exhibitions
to acquaint the public with Black artists. Art centers
were at Howard University, Langston University, Atlanta
Georgia, Richmond, Virginia, and New York. Other
agencies have cooperated with the Harmon Foundation in
widening public knowledge of Black art.

258.   Harris, Jessica B. "The Prolific Palette Jacob Lawrence." Encore, Vol. 4, November, 1974, pp. 52-53.

On May 16, 1974, Jacob Lawrence was honored by a two-
month retrospective showing of his works at Whitney
Museum. During the same month, Pope Paul VI hung one
of his paintings in the art gallery of the Vatican Museum. A biographical sketch of Mr. Lawrence is included.
Mr. Lawrence felt that Blacks should be exposed to more
art and they should be placed on the boards of art museums. A picture of Mr. Lawrence and one of his
poster designs are shown.

259.   Henderson, Rose. "First Nationwide Exhibit of Negro
Artists." Southern Workman, Vol. 57, March, 1928,
pp. 121-126.

The First Nationwide Exhibition of Negro Artists was
held at the Art Center in New York. Fifty-seven artists were represented with United States and some Car-
ribean artists participating. This show stressed the
humanizing influence of art as a factor which trans-
cends race prejudice. A list of winners and five of
the pieces are shown.

260.   _____. "Negro Artists in the Fifth Harmon Exhibition. Southern Workman, Vol. 62, April, 1933, pp. 175-
181.

The Art Center in New York was the scene of the Fifth
Annual Harmon Exhibition. Fifty-seven artists were
featured from the United States, Cuba, and the West
Indies. Among the winning artists were Sargent Johnson, Palmer Hayden, William Ellisworth Artis, James A.
Porter, and Earle Wilton Richardson. Pictures of each
winning art piece is shown and a short sketch of each
winning artist is given.

261. Hepburn, Dave. "Ellen Powell: Most Promising Young
      Artist." Sepia, Vol. 13, June, 1964, pp. 47-50.

      An emotional painter who draws from her environment
      and paints life as she sees it, Ms. Ellen Powell de-
      scribes herself as an expressionist painter who likes
      to paint people instead of landscapes. Pictures of Ms.
      Powell at work and one of her paintings are shown.

262. Herring, James V. "The American Negro as Craftsman
      and Artist." Crisis, Vol. 49, April, 1952, pp. 116-
      118.

      Gives insight into some of the earlier Negro craftsmen
      who have been neglected in previous literature. Tom
      Day was a cabinet maker as early as 1881 and was one
      such craftsman. Craftsmen were prominent during the
      Nineteenth Century in Philadelphia, Charleston, and
      New Orleans. Edward Bannister and Henry O. Tanner
      were painters during this period. Second generation
      artists include William E. Scott, Malvin Johnson, and
      Archibald Motley. Mr. Motley was better known. He
      had a one-man show in New York in 1928. His paintings
      on Negro culture in Africa and Haiti won him the Harmon
      Award and a Guggenheim Fellowship. A picture of Ho-
      ward University's art gallery is shown.

263. Holbrook, Francis C. "A Group of Negro Artists." Op-
      portunity, Vol. 1, July, 1923, pp. 221-231.

      List of recognized artists, sculptures, and illustra-
      tors such as Edward M. Bannister, Henry O. Tanner,
      William E. Scott, Edmonia Lewis, Meta Warrick Fuller,
      Laura Wheeler Waring, Augusta Savage, and Warren Smith.
      Brief biographical sketches plus a listing of some of
      the artists' works. A picture of one of Meta Warrick
      Fuller's sculptures is shown.

264. "Honoring Negro History." Art Design, Vol. 23, Feb-
      ruary 15, 1949, p. 20.

      Very few racial themes were present at the all Black
      exhibition at the RoKo Gallery honoring Negro History
      Week. Such artists as Charles White, Rose Piper,
      Claude Clarke, and others were on display.

265.   "Horizon." Crisis, Vol. 23, April, 1922, p. 273.

The works of Henry O. Tanner was among twenty-five
artists chosen to have works exhibited at the Twenty-
First International Art Exhbit. Eleven of his paint-
ings had been on exhibit at the Detroit Institute of
Arts and his works had been exhibited annually at the
Paris Salon since 1895. His painting, "The Raising of
Lazarus," won a medal and was purchased by the French
government for Luxembourg.

266.   "Horizon." Crisis, Vol. 26, May, 1923, p. 27.

Archibald J. Motley, Jr. had two paintings exhibited
at the Chicago Artists' Annual Exhibit at the Art Institute of Chicago.

267.   "Horizon." Crisis, Vol. 29, March, 1925, p. 223.

Edwin Augustus Harleston, a Negro painter, was commissioned to paint an oil portrait of Pierre S. DuPont
and was presented by the Negro citizens in Delaware
in appreciation for providing modern school buildings
for Negro children in the State. The portrait was
hung in the State House. The portrait was shown.
Also Mr. William Grenagi was commissioned by the
Frederick, Maryland Kiwanis Club to do an oil painting
of Francis Scott Key to be hung in the Key Hotel. The
portrait is shown.

268.   "Horizon." Crisis, Vol. 30, July, 1925, pp. 134-135.

Two prizes were won by Archibald Motley, Jr. at the
Chicago Artists' Exhibition. Mr. Motley specialized
in portraiture. A picture of Mr. Motley is shown plus
his painting, "The Grandmother," which was receiving
great attention.

269.   "Hugh Harrell." Freedomways, Vol. 3, Spring, 1963,
p. 168.

Previously a barber and seaman, Mr. Harrell developed
his early artistic abilities and was awarded a two-
year scholarship at the Brooklyn Museum of Art School.
Six of his black and white prints, dealing with women
are shown mostly.

270.   Hughes, Langston. "The Negro Artist and the Racial
Mountain." Nation, Vol. 122, June 23, 1926, pp. 692-
694.

The road to success for Black artists to produce a
racial art is rocky. Getting little encouragement
from neither Blacks nor Whites, with sharp criticism
from Blacks and unintentional bribes from Whites, Mr.
Hughes said that he hoped to see the works of Black

(Hughes, Langston)

painters who "paint and model the beauty of dark faces and create with new techniques the expressions of their own soul world." George S. Schuyler offered a different opinion in the June 16, 1926 issue of The Nation.

271.   "Hughie Lee-Smith." Crisis, Vol. 77, April, 1970, p. 163.

Biographical sketch of Mr. Lee-Smith who studied at the Cleveland Institute of Art. He has won many prizes and awards for his art and his works have been exhibited at such places as the Barnett-Aden Gallery, Detroit Institute, and the Museum of Modern Art. His works are in the permanent collections of Howard University, the University of Michigan, Detroit Institute of Art, etc.

272.   "In A Black Bind." Time, Vol. 97, April 12, 1971, p. 64.

Tells of how some Black artists pulled out of the Whitney Museum's, "Black Artists in America Exhibit." The Black Emergency Cultural Coalition had called for the museum to hire a Black cultural expert to help organize the show. Some Black artists stayed in the show and were caught in the crossfire.

273.   "In the Galleries - Romare Bearden." Arts Magazine, Vol. 39, November, 1964, p. 60.

Mr. Bearden's exhibit at the Cordier-Ekstrom Museum shows enlarged photographs of collages of cut-up photographs. The form is Cubist. Bearden and the people in his photographs are all Black.

274.   "Inside the Art Students' League." Our World, Vol. 10, July, 1955, pp. 68-74.

The leading independent art school, the Art Students' League, enrolls students on a month-to-month basis. Every since its founding in 1879, it has been open to Blacks. Pictures of some of the Black students featured and some of their works are shown.

275.   "Introduction to the Negro in American History." Arts Magazine, Vol. 44, September/October, 1969, p. 58.

Nine paintings by Jacob Lawrence from the series, "The Negro Migration," are shown among the entries in this exhibit on Negro art. Organized by Middleton A. Harris, the show was based on the loss of personal status and the struggle to regain it. The collection consisted of photographs, drawings, rare books, posters, newspapers, paintings, and craft objects.

276.   Jackson, Esther. "Why Harlem Needs a Cultural Center."
       Negro Digest, Vol. 15, June, 1966, pp. 76-81.

       Dr. Jackson felt that the Harlem Cultural Center
       would provide the Black community with an effective
       way to desegregate the arts not only in New York, but
       throughout the country. She lists five specific
       functions of the center.

277.   "Jacob Lawrence." Ebony, Vol. 6, April, 1951, pp. 73-
       76, 78.

       After a patient at Hillside Mental Hospital, Jacob
       Lawrence produced several paintings portraying life
       in an insane asylum. Art critics felt these paintings
       portraying life were emotionally richer, technically
       more advanced, and socially more signigicant than his
       previous works. Between 1940 and 1950, was his most
       productive period when he did 250 paintings which were
       rapidly purchased by art collectors and museums. When
       asked why he chose to do Negro themes, he said that,
       "I can only express the people and the class of which
       I am a part." Three pictures of him at work, with his
       family, and his agent are shown. Forty-seven of his
       paintings are included.

278.   "James A. Porter." Opportunity, Vol. 11, February,
       1933, pp. 46-47.

       Biographical sketch of James A. Porter, a Howard
       graduate, art instructor, and later Head of the Art
       Department. Lists his most impressive works and
       where his works have been exhibited. He also designed
       stage settings for plays at Howard University. Three
       of his paintings are shown.

279.   Johnson, James Weldon. "Race Prejudice and the Negro
       Artist." Harper's Magazine, Vol. 157, November, 1928,
       pp. 769-776.

       Looks at the race problem on the development of Negro
       artists in all fields. In looking at artistic achieve-
       ment, Mr. Johnson noted that the Black man has not won
       marked distinction in the decade of the 1920s or
       earlier when the works of Henry O. Tanner, Edmonia
       Lewis, and Meta Warrick Fuller gained prominence. He
       notes the recent progress of W. E. Scott and Archibald
       J. Motley.

280.   Jones, Lois Mailou. "An Artist Grows Up in America."
       The Afro-American Woman's Journal, Vol. 3, Summer/Fall,
       1942, p. 23.

(Jones, Lois Mailou)

Autobiographical sketch by Ms. Jones and notes the
role of the artist during the war years. The Artists'
Guild of Washington, DC was formed to aid the nation
in national defense and other programs.

281. Jones, Walter. "To Black Artists." Arts Magazine,
      Vol. 44, April, 1970, pp. 16-18, 20.

      Short sketch on William Williams, who moved to New
      York and later became a successful painter. Mr. Jones
      had a poorly written article using a great deal of pro-
      fanity and jive language to convey his message.

282. "Karamu House of Cleveland Has Art Exhibit in New
      York." Opportunity, Vol. 20, February, 1942, p. 59.

      The Associated American Artists held an exhibit at its
      Galleries of paintings, drawings, ceramics, and sculp-
      ture produced by its students. Founded in 1915, Kara-
      mu House trained the creative abilities of Black art
      students. It gave the students a chance to become
      known and to tell the story of their sufferings, dis-
      satisfactions, aspirations, and ambitions to the world.

283. Kaufman, Arthur. "The Newly Born Lamb." Crisis, Vol.
      72, June/July, 1965, pp. 363, 396.

      Mr. Kaufman's painting, "The Newly Born Lamb," was
      donated to the NAACP by an anonymous donor. Mr. Kauf-
      man goes on to explain that he painted the picture be-
      cause it was a symbol of love and his belief in the
      Bill of Rights and to show others that the Bill of
      Rights is working in America. The painting is shown
      in the article.

284. Kendrick, Ruby Moyse. "Art at Howard University: An
      Appreciation." Crisis, Vol. 39, November, 1932, pp.
      348-349.

      The author feels that Howard University would become
      one of the distinguished art centers in the country.
      The Art Gallery opened in April 7, 1930 in the reno-
      vated chapel basement. Credit for the success of the
      gallery was given to James V. Herring who founded the
      Art Gallery and is pictured in the article. Many di-
      versified exhibits have been displayed. In addition
      to exhibits of paintings, sculpture, craft work, lec-
      tures have also been done by prominent people in art.
      The Art Gallery sparked such an interest in art that
      the Friends of Art was formed which sponsored a pro-
      ject in art appreciation.

285.   Kerr, Adelaide. "A Record-Breaking Exhibit (Library)
        By a Group of Artists (Black)." Wilson Library Bulle-
        tin, Vol. 43, April, 1969, pp. 756-759.

        A "Black Artists' Exhibit" at the Inglewood (Califor-
        nia) Public Library proved a huge success. A panel
        discussion by Black artists, "What Art Means to the
        Black Community," opened the session. Fifty paintings,
        large abstracts, portraits, landscapes, and medal and
        wood sculptures were included. Six of the art pieces
        are shown and three of patrons touring the exhibit.

286.   Kleinhans, Lee. "New Eight Cent Postage Stamp Honors
        Black Artist." Sepia, Vol. 23, March, 1974, pp. 62-
        66, 68.

        On September 10, 1973, a commemorative postage stamp
        was issued honoring Black artist Henry O. Tanner.
        The picture on the stamp was designed from a picture
        by Tanner's first art teacher, Thomas Eakins. A
        biographical sketch on Tanner's life and artistic ac-
        complishments is given. A picture of the stamp, one
        of Mr. Tanner, and five of his works are shown.

287.   Lane, James W. "Afro-American Art on Both Continents."
        Art News, Vol. 40, October 15-31, 1941, p. 25.

        The author notes the exhibit by McMillan, Inc. on Afro-
        American art. Tells of the works of William Carter,
        Romare Bearden, Loraine Williams, John Carlis, and
        other mostly unknown Black artists whose works contri-
        buted to the exhibit. Along with pictures were Afri-
        can sculptures from the Belgian Congo, the Ivory
        Coast, and Gabon. It was stated that "those sculp-
        tures complement in an appropriate manner the art
        Negroes from our own hemisphere and show how they
        have always had their own highly original artistic
        sense which they keep uncontaminated."

288.   Lawrence, Jacob. "The Artist Responds." Crisis,
        Vol. 77, August/September, 1970, pp. 266-267.

        Jacob Lawrence was the recipient of the Fifty-Fifth
        Spingarn Medal, "in tribute to the compelling power of
        his works . . . and in salute to his unswerving com-
        mitment, not only to his art, but to his Black brother
        within the context of hope for a single society." Mr.
        Lawrence spoke of the efforts of Black artists and
        their supporters to create a greater awareness and ex-
        posure of Black artists. He thanked the Black com-
        munity and the NAACP and other organizations which
        encouraged and supported the cultural endeavors of the
        Black community. He said "between us all - the Black
        community, the Black scholar, and the practicing Black
        artist - let us hope to keep alive a vital art prac-
        ticed by Black artists."

289.   Lawson, Edward. "He Crashed the Color Line." Op-
       portunity, Vol. 17, February, 1939, pp. 52-53.

       Perry R. Watkins, a Black artist, was the first Black
       to become a scenic designer on the Broadway stage when
       he was assigned to prepare the sets for "Mamba's
       Daughters." He pioneered in provided a new color syn-
       thesis of background, costume, and light for the Negro
       on the stage. A short biographical sketch is included
       and a picture of Mr. Watkins is shown.

290.   "Leading Negro Artist." Ebony, Vol. 18, September,
       1963, pp. 131-132, 134, 136, 138, 140.

       Notes the creative abilities of several Black art-
       ists: Jacob Lawrence, Hale Woodruff, Charles Alston,
       Romare Bearden, Aaron Douglas, Norman Lewis, John Big-
       gers, Richmond Barthe, Richard Hunt, Charles White,
       Hughie Lee-Smith, Selma Burke, John Hollingsworth,
       Ernest Crichlow, Ellis Wilson, John Wilson, Humbert
       Howard, William Artis, James L. Wills, and Eugene
       Grigsby. A picture of each artist with one of their
       works is included.

291.   "Leading Young Artists." Ebony, Vol. 13, April, 1958,
       pp. 33-38.

       A study of the American art scene in 1958 revealed
       that Negro artists were producing work of intense
       vigor, breadth of content and stylistic variety.
       Ebony chose twenty-four artists as representatives of
       the gifted group of Black artists who were making a
       notable contribution. Ranging from realism to bold
       abstractionalism, their subject matter was not purely
       racial. Pictures of each artist and their works are
       shown.

292.   "Lee Jack Morton." Freedomways, Vol. 6, Spring, 1966,
       p. 192.

       The art of Mr. Morton was featured in this fifth anni-
       versary issue of Freedomways. An active artist in the
       Freedom Movement, he designed the voter registration
       poster for SCLC and he illustrated the Mississippi is-
       sue of Freedomways done in Spring, 1965. Two oil can-
       vasses, one his self portrait, and one pastel is fea-
       tured.

293.   Lester, William R. "Henry O. Tanner, Exile for Art's
       Sake." Alexander's Magazine, Vol. 7, December, 1908,
       pp. 69-73.

       Beginning his studies in France in 1891, he had some
       paintings accepted at the Paris Salon. Most of his
       paintings are of biblical subjects. In Paris, Mr.
       Tanner did not find the racial obstacles which barred

(Lester, William R.)

him from success in his own country.

294.   Lewis, Theophilus.   "Primer Lesson for Harlem Critics."
        The Messenger, Vol. 7, June, 1925, p. 230.

        Mr. Lewis feels that the critic who appraises the art
        of the Black must have a clear understanding of the
        spiritual and sociological conditions that art seeks
        to interpret.   The task of the Black artist is to ob-
        serve his environment and reveal its meaning in a
        graceful manner.

295.   _____.   "The Frustration of Negro Art."   The
        Catholic World, Vol. 155, April, 1942, pp. 51-57.

        Notes the many social, economic, and political pro-
        blems of Negroes, especially in the field of art.
        Author feels that the status of the Negro compels the
        Negro artist to work under an economic hardship and
        lack of appreciation and paying public to support them.
        He goes on to talk about the problems of Negroes in
        literature, music, theatre, and other performing arts.
        In conclusion, the author felt that the Negro can
        hardly be expected to perform the miracle of creating
        mature painting or a living literature until his cul-
        ture causes a demand for those arts within his race.

296.   Lockard, Jon Onye.   "An Ideology for Black Artists."
        First World, Vol. 2, Spring, 1978, pp. 42-44.

        Author notes that the Black artists must continually
        fight oppression if their art is to survive.   They must
        have the courage to incorporate new art forms, new
        spaces, and volumes, and new cultural values which
        involve through critical selection and establish na-
        tional and local organizations geared toward encourag-
        ing that criticism.   Two pictures of artists at the
        Twentieth Anniversary of the National Conference of
        Artists and a poster from an art exhibit in Atlanta
        are shown.   Mr. Lockard teaches at the University and
        Washtenaw Community College.   He is also director of
        the Academy of Creative Thought and Second Vice Presi-
        dent of the National Conference of African American
        Artists.

297.   "Lois M. Jones Painting Award."   Women United, Vol. 9,
        August, 1949, p. 26.

        Ms. Jones was awarded the 1949 John Hope Purchase
        Award for the best landscape at the Eighth Atlanta Uni-
        versity Exhibition of Paintings, Sculpture, and Prints
        by Negro Artists.   The same painting also had won
        first prize in oil painting at the 1947 National Mu-
        seum Exhibit.

298. Long, Fern. "A Cultural Operation Crossroads." _Crisis_,
      Vol. 53, December, 1946, p. 367-368, 380.

      Tells of an exhibit at the Cleveland Museum of Art en-
      titled, "Portraits of Outstanding Americans of Negro
      Origin." The twenty-seven portraits were done by
      Betsy Graves Reyneau and Laura Wheeler Waring. Notes
      the many people and organizations in Chicago who worked
      to make the exhibit a success. The Cleveland Public
      Library displayed photographs of the portraits plus
      books about each person which was almost as popular as
      the exhibit itself.

299. "Lorenzo Harris." _Opportunity_, Vol. 12, July, 1934,
      p. 222.

      Mr. Harris did the center drawing in this issue of
      Opportunity. It was of Crispus Attucks, the first
      martyr of the Revolutionary War. Mr. Harris engaged
      in doing a series of historical studies of the Ameri-
      can Negro. He studied at the Philadelphia Academy of
      Fine Arts.

300. Louchheim, Aline B. "Art In An Insane Asylum." _Negro
      Digest_, Vol. 9, February, 1951, pp. 14-19.

      While a patient at a mental hospital in Queens, New
      York, Jacob Lawrence did eleven paintings on the moods
      and routines of life at the hospital. They were exhi-
      bited at the Downtown Gallery in New York. Other
      interesting facts on his life were portrayed and a
      picture is included.

301. Lowenfeld, Viktor. "New Negro Art in America." _De-
      sign_, Vol. 46, September, 1944, pp. 20-21, 29.

      Author lists three psychological factors which in-
      fluence the art of the Negro: (1) Heritage of the
      Negro - author feels that the Negro has lost his direct
      relationship to his African ancestors but there is
      still a psychological relationship to this culture,
      even when negatively expressed; (2) The special status
      of the Negro in America has had a positive and nega-
      tive effect on the development of a specific Negro art;
      and (3) The influence of Western Civilization inhibited
      the development of a genuine Negro art. Four paint-
      ings are shown.

302. Marc, Warren. "Alston: American Artist." _Crisis_,
      Vol. 76, February, 1969, pp. 93-97.

      The contemporary American artist, Charles Alston had
      works exhibited in all major museums in the country.
      He is represented in several permanent collections in-
      cluding the Metropolitan Museum and the NAACP. His
      show at the Gallery of Modern Art sponsored by Fair-

(Marc, Warren)

leigh Dickinson University was the first in a series
of exhibits by Black artists at the museum. Mr. Alston's works included fifty-four of his paintings and
three of his sculptures. His sculpture in three different media were: mahogany, bronze, and limestone.
Mr. Alston's picture and five pieces of his work are
shown.

303.   "Marine Combat Artist." Ebony, Vol. 26, May, 1971,
        pp. 104-106, 108, 110.

Staff Sgt. James A. Fairfax, the only Black among six-
ty-seven participating artists in the United States
Marine Corps Combat Art Program. He captured war
scenes of the Vietnam War. The pictures from this art
program were to be exhibited at museums throughout the
country. Fifty of his pictures, plus pictures of Sgt.
Fairfax at work were shown. Some of Sgt. Fairfax's
paintings have been exhibited at the National Urban
League Conference.

304.   Mashek, Joseph. "Black Artists, Visual Arts Gallery."
        Artforum, Vol. 9, September, 1970, pp. 79-80.

In a group show entitled, "Black Artists, 1970," sixteen artists were featured. Although the show was
billed as the first professional Black art exhibit,
the writer feels that it was not. He stated that the
artists have a problem in relation to the culture at
large, that is, the romantic identification with the
present life vs the values of the urban civilization
and that the works were not a quality to be termed
professional. None of the pieces were shown in the
article.

305.   Merry, Ruth C. "Art Talent and Racial Background."
        Journal of Educational Research, Vol. 32, September,
        1938, pp. 17-22.

A study done by art teachers to show the relationship
of art talent to racial background. Letters were sent
to artists to get their judgment of the important com-
prising art talent. Children of all nationalities
were studied finding that Negro children were average,
Russian children below average, and American and
Italian children above average. Study has many draw-
backs. Figures showed that only eight-one out of
one thousand three hundred ninety-three children were
studied and that was not a high enough percentage to
evaluate effectively.

306.   "Methodist in Paris." Time, Vol. 94, July 11, 1969,
        p. 58.

Although Henry O. Tanner was more popular in Paris than in the United States, the National Collection of Fine Arts wanted to correct the oversight. They sponsored a retrospective exhibit of eighty of his works done from his student days to those done shortly before his death. Two paintings, "Banjo Lesso," and "Abraham's Oak" are shown.

307.   Montgomery, Evangeline J. "Southern California Black Art Activities." Phase II, Vol. 1, Spring, 1970, pp. 9-13, 32-33.

A chronological listing of new galleries, art shows, and Black studies programs in the California area between 1962 and 1970.

308.   _____. "Black Art Activities." Phase II, Vol. 2, Summer, 1970, pp. 10-12.

A discussion of Black artists and their activities in the Southern California area.

309.   Moore, Trevor W. "Sanguinary Saga." Christian Century, Vol. LXXXVIII, July 14, 1971, pp. 864-865.

An exhibition, "Some American History," was on display at Rice University in Houston. It showed the works of both Black and White artists. It was a collection of drawings, posters, collages, paintings, mixed media pieces, and twenty odd giant sculptures. To compliment the show's total effect, a multimedia installation echoed the sounds and places of Black life (roars of mobs, excerpts from speeches of Malcolm X, African and blues music, etc.). Two pictures from the exhibition are shown.

310.   Mora, Elizabeth Catlett. "The Negro People on American Art." Freedomways, Vol. 1, Spring, 1964, pp. 74-80.

Notes the two great periods in Negro Art in the United States: The Negro Renaissance and the National Conference of Negro Artists. A third period of Negro art can be initiated but commercial and political exploitation must be avoided. Through the National Conference, the Negro can make a major contribution to the struggle for full equality. Written article by one of the major Black women artists.

311.   Moss, Robert F. "The Arts in Black America." Saturday Review, Vol. 58, November 15, 1975, pp. 12-19.

In terms of fine arts most political commentaries have appeared in ghetto murals and huge hieroglyphics of protest and outrage. Although racial elements seem the dominant theme of Black artists there are some

(Moss, Robert F.)

working outside this area.

312.   Motley, Willard F. "Negro Art in Chicago." _Opportunity_, Vol. 18, January, 1940, pp. 19-22.

Comments on the exhibit at Hull House by young beginning Negro artists. Some of the artists on display were Charles White, Charles Davis, William Carter, Henry Avery, Ramon Gabriel, Charles Sebree, Earl Walker, Fred Hollingsworth, and Eldzier Cortor. Mr. Motley visited the studios of some of these artists and sheds some light into why and what they painted. Two paintings, and one by Eldzier Cortor and one by William Carter are shown.

313.   "Munich Portrait." _Our World_, Vol. 10, September, 1955, pp. 42-44.

Widely known as the "Negro with the Troylean Hat," William Billie Pulliam discovered the German art centers and became a leading artist in Munich. Several pictures of him at work and his family are shown.

314.   Munro, Thomas. "Primitive Negro Scultpure." _Opportunity_, Vol. 4, May, 1926, pp. 150-152.

Author feels that to appreciate Negro art one must appreciate sculptural design. Mr. Munro goes on to describe the rhythmic sequence and three-dimensional solidarity in art and notes that the Negroes' mastery of sculpture is demonstrated by a complex unity of organization and a delicate precision of detail.

315.   Murray, Freeman H. M. "Representations of the Emancipation in American Art." _Opportunity_, Vol. 2, April, 1924, pp. 115-118.

Looks at the attempts of American artists - sculptors and painters - to give objective treatment to the theme of emancipation. Also attempts to indicate the difficulties in the portrayal of this abstract theme. Talks at length of John Qunicy Adams Ward's statuette, "The Freedman" which met with high acclaim from the critics and general public. A picture of the statuette is included.

316.   "The Museum: Its Role and Responsibility." _Art Gallery_, April, 1970, pp. 60-63.

The editors of _Art Gallery_ invited the directors of establishment museums to voice their opinions on the roles and responsibilities of their museums vis-a-vis the Black community. Some respondents included Jan van der Marck (Museum of Contemporary Art, Chicago),

Henri Ghent (Community Art Gallery), and Thomas S.
Beuchner (Brooklyn Museum). General opinion was that
Black artists have been neglected and the Black art-
ists are a token gesture.

317. "Museums and the Ghetto." Newsweek, Vol. 76, August 17, 1970, p. 93.

A Black artist, Tom Lloyd, backed by the director of
the New York Metropolitan Museum, secured a $29,000
grant to survey ghetto residents on what they want
the art museums to provide. He found that they want
independent cultural centers of their own. Mrs. Lee
Kimche secured a $50,000 grant to launch new art pro-
grams to reach minority groups. Notes the Anacostia
Neighborhood Museum in Washington, DC, and "Project
Outreach" in Detroit as examples of new ghetto art programs. But critics did feel that more art programs
should take place at larger museums and not limit it
to developing small art centers in ghetto neighbor-
hoods.

318. "Museums Buy Pippin." Art Digest, Vol. 15, March 1,
1941, p. 13.

Two museums acquired works by "primitive" Negro art-
ist Horace Pippin. The Barnes Foundation acquired
"Suppertime," and the Philadelphia Museum purchased
"End of the War."

319. "Music and Art." Crisis, Vol. 4, June, 1912, p. 63.

Some paintings of William E. Scott were accepted for
the spring exhibit of the Paris Salon. He was working
in the studio of the great Black artist, Henry O.
Tanner.

320. "Music and Art." Crisis, Vol. 5, February, 1913,
pp. 169-170.

The Carlton Avenue branch of the Brooklyn YMCA featured an exhibit by Black artists. One artist whose
works were praised was Ernest Braxton who had seven
pictures in oil and a series of studies in Black and
white. Some other artists exhibited were Louise R.
Latimer, G. E. Livingston, Walter T. Brown and others.

321. "Music and Art." Crisis, Vol. 6, July, 1913, p. 119.

Cloyd L. Boykin had an exhibit of thirty paintings at
the Twentieth Century Club in Boston. Mr. Boykins
was studying at the Boston Museum of Fine Art. The
Boston Globe noted that all the sketches showed a
splendid grasp of the fundamentals in both drawing and
color.

322.   "Music and Art." Crisis, Vol. 7, January, 1914, p.
        114.

        William E. Scott painted a mural decoration for a
        grammar school in Indianapolis. The painting illu-
        strated the Mother Goose rhyme "The Old Lady in a
        Shoe." Black children were used as models for the
        characters.

323.   "Music and Art." Crisis, Vol. 8, June, 1914, p. 61.

        Henry O. Tanner had two canvasses on exhibit at the
        Society of French Artists, the largest exhibit in the
        world including several paintings and sculptures. Mr.
        Tanner's work was the best he had done and was full of
        religious feelings.

324.   "Music and Art." Crisis, Vol. 15, December, 1917,
        p. 85.

        An exhibition of pictures by Black artists including
        some children, was held at the Coady Art Galleries in
        New York. The exhibit was sponsored by the American
        Circle of Negro War Relief.

325.   "Music and Art." Crisis, Vol. 19, March, 1920, p.
        279.

        Aaron Douglas, the only Black student in the Art De-
        partment of Nebraska State University, was selected
        from among fifty students to do a charcoal sketch of
        General Pershing.

326.   "Music and Art." Crisis, Vol. 21, April, 1921, p.
        271.

        The works of Henry O. Tanner were exhibited at the
        John Wanamaker Gallery in Philadelphia. They in-
        cluded "The Wise and Foolish Virgins," "The Flight
        Into Egypt," and "Annunciation."

327.   "Music and Art." Crisis, Vol. 35, May, 1928, p. 163.

        John T. Hailstalk held his first exhibit at the Thomas
        Russell Galleries in New York. Albert A. Smith held
        an exhibit of his paintings, lithographs, and draw-
        ings at the School of Design and Liberal Arts in New
        York. A picture of Anna Washington Derry is shown.
        It was done by Laura Wheeler Waring and won the Harmon
        Award for painting.

328.   MacLean, M. D. "Richard Lonsdale Brown." Crisis,
        Vol. 3, April, 1912, pp. 255-257.

        Biographical sketch of the rough life Mr. Brown had in
        pursuing his career in art. With help of Mr. George

(MacLean, M. D.)

deForest Brush, who took him as a pupil, and took him
to New Hampshire to paint the landscape there. These
paintings were exhibited on Fifth Avenue in New York
City.

329.   McCausland, Elizabeth.   "Jacob Lawrence." Magazine of
       Art, Vol. 38, November, 1945, pp. 25-254.

       Tells of the exhibit on Coast Guard life at the Museum
       of Modern Art which Jacob Lawrence did while he served
       in the Coast Guard. He painted troops embarking, com-
       ing home, in their bunks, at mess, etc. because he
       wanted the public to see what was going on in the
       Coast Guard. A short biographical sketch of Mr. Law-
       rence is included. A comparison of the Migration
       Series of Mr. Lawrence is included. A comparison of
       the Migration Series, the Harlem Series, and the
       Coast Guard Series of pictures all done by him show
       that he has grown higher in key, more brilliant in
       color. Nine pictures from all three series are shown
       along with a picture of Mr. Lawrence. Article shows
       the continued growth of this artist.

330.   "National Art Week Observances and Negro Artists."
       Opportunity, Vol. 19, November, 1941, p. 345.

       The work of Black artists received special attention
       during the National Art Week. Tuskegee Institute cele-
       brated by opening new art rooms in the George Washing-
       ton Carver Museum. The WPA listed 17,397 Black stu-
       dents enrolled in the WPA Art Program classes.

331.   "Negro Annual." Art Digest, Vol. 20, April 15, 1946,
       p. 3.

       The Fifth Annual Exhibit of Negro Artists at Atlanta
       University was being held until April 28. The show
       gives encouragement to minorities whose paintings are
       not a question of race but of social and cultural
       environment.

332.   "Negro Annual." Art News, Vol. 42, April 15-30,
       1943, p. 6.

       Notes the Second Annual Art Exhibit at Atlanta Univer-
       sity. Seventy-five oils and water colors were dis-
       played. All winning art work became part of the uni-
       versity's permanent collection. A picture of the Two
       Hundred Fifty Dollar John Hope Prize, "Black Soldier,"
       was shown. A list of all prize winners was given.

333.   "Negro Art." Crisis, Vol. 32, September, 1926,
       pp. 245-246.

Articles by George S. Schuyler and Langston Hughes
were published in a national magazine. Some comments
from both are cited below. Mr. Schuyler felt there
was no pure Negro art. Since the Negro responds to
the same environment influences as Whites, he should
not be expected to produce art dissimilar to Whites.
Mr. Hughes felt differently. He felt that the Negro
aped the White man and did not realize his own worth
in producing a unique art form.

334.   "Negro Art Annual." Art Digest, Vol. 16, May 1, 1942,
p. 9.

Atlanta University presented the First Annual Exhibit
of Oils and Water Colors by Negro Artists. In his
catalogue foreward, Alain Locke said, the exhibit had
a peculiar timeliness. One painting, Harmonica
Player, is shown.

335.   "Negro Art At RoKo." Art Digest, Vol. 20, February 1,
1946, p. 10.

In commemoration of Negro History Week, the RoKo Gallery held an exhibition by Black artists. Sales bene-
fited the Washington Carver School.

336.   "Negro Art Exhibit." Southern Workman, Vol. 53,
April, 1924, pp. 149-150.

Annual exhibits of Black artists are held in Washington, DC, Boston, and New York. One exhibit in New
York by the Library Round Table consisted of oils and
water colors. Some of the persons exhibited were
E. A. Harleston, Laura Wheeler, A. J. Motley, Louise
R. Latimer, and Charles Osborne. Describes the works
by each artist.

337.   "Negro Art from Cleveland's Karamu House." Art Digest,
Vol. 16, January 15, 1942, p. 19.

Associated American Artists held an exhibit on Negro
art at the Karamu House, a free cultural art center
for Negroes. The show reflected restraint, no outstanding racial characteristics and the effect of good
teaching and considerable promise. More emphasis was
on prints and the water colors were characterized by
sound design. A picture of three employees of Karamu
House are shown.

338.   "Negro Art in Brooklyn." Crisis, Vol. 39, August,
1932, p. 259.

Twelve oil paintings by James Lesesne Wells and one
large modern canvas by Archibald Motley, Jr., were on
display at the Brooklyn Museum.

339.   "Negro Art Prizes." Art News, Vol. 43, May 1-14, 1944, p. 7.

John Farrar won first prize at the Atlanta University Third Annual Exhibition of Paintings, Sculpture, and Prints by Negro Artists. A student at the Art Students League, Farrar had been doing water colors since age five. One hundred seventy works were in the exhibition.

340.   "Negro Art Scores Without Double Standards." Art Digest, Vol. 19, February 1, 1945, p. 8.

An exhibit entitled, "The Negro Artist Comes of Age," was on display at the Albany Institute of History and Art as a tribute to the creative contributions of Negroes. Forty-three artists were represented. The article notes that Negro art dates back to Africa and not when they arrived as slaves. Also noted the contributions of the Harmon Foundation and the financial help of the Carnegie Corporation in furthering Negro art.

341.   "Negro Art Show." Art News, Vol. 43, July 1-31, 1944, pp. 6-7.

An exhibition of the G Place Gallery in Washington, DC was called the "most impressive display of paintings by contemporary Negro Artists." The show had been presented at Hampton Institute and the Baltimore Museum and featured such new artists as Jacob Lawrence. It was noted that patrons may want to regard such works as an integral part of all Americans rather than as a racial manifestation which a segregated exhibition implied.

342.   "Negro Art Show." Crisis, Vol. 76, March, 1969, pp. 132-133.

The NAACP sponsored the first major gallery exhibition on Negro artists in many years at the Lee Nordness Gallery in New York. Works of the following artists were shown: Arthur Coppedge, Norman Lewis, Selrath Hines, Charles McGee, Carroll Sockwell, Alma Thomas, Walter Williams, etc. This article names some relatively unknown artists.

343.   "Negro Artist Comes of Age." Art News, Vol. 43, February 1-14, 1945, pp. 16, 29-30.

The Albany Institute of History and Art held an exhibit entitled, "The Negro Artist Comes of Age." Thirty-one artists were represented. Themes varied but most dealt with social sympathy and social protest. A general overview of Black achievement is given.

344.   "Negro Artists." Art News, Vol. 47, February, 1949, p. 47.

This article notes the opening of an exhibit by Negro artists at the RoKo Galleries in honor of Negro History Week. Paintings, sculptures, and prints by fifteen artists were exhibited. Lists some of the artists and their works.

345.   "Negro Artists Reveal Genius in Trenton Show." Art Digest, Vol. 9, April 15, 1935, p. 19.

The New Jersey State Museum was the site of an exhibition of Negro artists. Rhythmic lines and form were achieved with utmost simplicity by such artists as Augusta Savage, James Porter, and Richmond Barthe. Also unveiled were designs for a mural project at the One Hundred Thirty-Fifth Branch of the New York Public Library by Aaron Douglas.

346.   "Negro Artists Show." Art News, Vol. 43, January 1-14, 1945, p. 9.

Notes the upcoming exhibit at the Albany Institute of History entitled, "The Negro Artist Comes of Age." It was the first large scale attempt to bring together and analyze the contributions of Black artists. The catalogue contained an introductory history of the works by Black artists, biographical sketches and reproductions of works.

347.   "Negro Artists: Their Works Win Top United States Honors." Life, Vol. 21, July 22, 1946, p. 62.

Notes the achievements of Black artists from the 1700s to the present. Cites the annual exhibition sponsored by the Harmon Foundation from 1928-1935 which encourages Black artists and the Federal Arts Project in 1934 which gave jobs and exhibitions to Black artists. Twelve pieces of sculpture and paintings by various artists are shown.

348.   "Negroes Exhibit Their Art." Pictures on Exhibit, Vol. 2, February, 1939, pp. 8-9.

The Harmon Foundation sponsored an exhibition of Negro art at the Baltimore Museum of Art. One painting, "All Day Meeting," by Malvin Johnson is shown.

349.   "Negro GI in Belgium." Sepia, Vol. 12, January, 1963, pp. 32-34.

Robert R. D'Hue has had some of his abstract works accepted by the Museum of Art in LUIK, and has given exhibitions in Belgium, Holland, France, and Luxemburg. Pictures of his family and some of his works are shown.

350. "Negro History Week." Student Life, Vol. 7, February,
      1941, p. 23.

      Student Life observed Negro History Week by presenting
      examples of Negro art which was part of the American
      Negro Exhibition. This first Negro World's Fair com-
      memorated the Seventy-Fifth anniversary of the Thir-
      teenth Amendment and gave proof of the contributions
      of the Negro since coming to America. Six paintings
      are shown.

351. "Negro in Art." Art News, Vol. 40, December 15-31,
      1941, p. 24.

      Notes the exhibition of American Negro art at the
      Downtown Gallery. Shows a cross-section of Negro a-
      chievement through the Nineteenth and Twentieth Cen-
      turies. Such artists as Horace Pippin, William Carter,
      and Charles Alston are discussed and a picture by
      Romare Bearden is shown. A tinge of racial overtones
      is noted when it was stressed that the Negro artist
      uses a wilder, more exotic color in his work than
      White artists.

352. "Negro in Art." Magazine of Art, Vol. 35, April, 1942,
      p. 147.

      Howard University's Art Department hosted a regional
      conference of the College Art Association. It also
      marked the Seventy-Fifth Anniversary of the founding
      of Howard University and also the Thirty-Seventh Anni-
      versary of the teaching of art at Howard University
      which began in 1905, along with the success of the
      Howard University Art Gallery founded in 1927. Two
      pictures from the exhibit are shown.

353. "Negro Prize Winners." Art Digest, Vol. 4, January 1,
      1930, p. 11.

      The Harmon Foundation sponsored an exhibition of works
      by Negro artists at International House in New York Art
      critic, William Averbach-Levy said of the show, "their
      paintings were more like their White fellows. They
      usually have White teachers who pressure them to
      abandon their racial themes in art."

354. "Negro Winners." Art Digest, Vol. 20, May 1, 1946, p.
      11.

      Lists winners of the Fifth Annual Exhibition of Paint-
      ings, Sculpture, and Prints by Negro Artists. Some
      winners included Joseph Delaney, Charles White, Ellis
      Wilson, Richmond Barthe, Elizabeth Catlett, Leonard
      Cooper, Franklin M. Sands, Wilmer Jennings and Roy de

Carava.

355. "Negro World's Fair." Newsweek, Vol. XVI, September 9, 1940, p. 20.

The American Negro Exposition in Chicago featured the accomplishments of the Negro in art, drama, agriculture, labor, science, and industry. A picture of Elizabeth Catlett's, "Negro Mother and Child," is shown.

356. "Negroes Sponsor Own Art." Art Digest, Vol. 6, June 1, 1932, p. 7.

Dallas was the site of the First Negro Art Exhibit ever held in the South or Southwest. Sponsored by the Dallas Federation of Colored Women's Clubs, the show had paintings, drawings, and crafts.

357. "New Yorkers Win Honors at Atlanta Show." Art Digest, Vol. 25, April 15, 1951, p. 13.

New Yorkers won four awards at the Tenth Annual Exhibition of Negro Artists at Atlanta University. Winners were Merton D. Simpson, Hale A. Woodruff, William Artis, and S. Charles White.

358. "Nineteen Young Americans." Life, Vol. 28, March 20, 1950, pp. 82-93.

Of the nineteen artists featured, one was Black - Eldzier Cortor. He studied in Chicago and won a Guggenheim Fellowship to paint in the West Indies. His painting, "The Room Number Five," is one of the many he has done on Gullah Negroes.

359. "O Richard Reid, Portraitist." Opportunity, Vol. 6, February, 1928, p. 51.

His portrait of Charles S. Johnson won honorable mention from the Harmon Foundation. Mr. Reid also had an exhibit at the One Hundred Thirty-Fifth Branch of the New York Library, the Society of Independent Artists, and the Anderson Galleries. He has received favorable reviews by art critics and some French art magazines have carried reproductions of his works. Mr. Reid's portrait of John Barrymore as "Hamlet" is shown.

360. "Object: Diversity." Time, Vol. 95, April 6, 1970, pp. 80-87.

This article looks at eight Black artists whose works are distinctly Black. Sparsely represented in museums and private collections, Black artists are now painting on street walls to get their messages across.

The works of Dana Chandler, Jr., Malcolm Bailey, Melvin Edwards, Richard Hunt, David Hammons, Sam Gilliam, David Johnson, and Joe Overstreet are discussed. Pictures of each artist and some of their works are shown. Four other street wall pictures are also shown.

361.   "Old Medium, New Message." Ebony, Vol. 27, December, 1971, pp. 33-36, 38, 40, 42.

Douglas Phillips uses contemporary designs for his stained glass window designs. He does abstract and impressionist designs. He does the designing and his wife and staff do the actual work. Thirteen pictures of Mr. Phillips, his staff, and his stained glass designs are shown.

362.   O'Neal, Frederick. "The Arts in Our Society: A Re-Evaluation of the Arts and the Artist." CLA Journal, Vol. 12, September, 1968, pp. 10-18.

This article cites the need for more interest in all forms of art and gives examples of some things done to support and utilize the arts. The author notes the recent involvement of labor and business groups in furthering the interest in the arts. He notes the work of the Business Committee for the Arts, and the National Foundation on the Arts and Humanities.

363.   "On Young Negro Artists." Opportunity, Vol. 1, January, 1923, pp. 16-18.

Two exhibits, one in New York and one in Boston, served to foster Black art. The New York exhibit promoted the works of young unknown art students. Most emphasis was on general artistic themes. Oils, water-colors, and etchings were on display. The Boston exhibit covered the graphic arts and also music. Six paintings from the two exhibits are shown.

364.   "One Man's Show." Our World, Vol. 9, May, 1954, pp. 67-69.

Ellis Wilson held his third one-man show at an art gallery in New York. Most of his materials show the rhythm, color, and charm of Haiti. Several of his paintings are shown plus pictures of patrons viewing his works.

365.   "Our Cover Artist." Opportunity, Vol. 19, January, 1941, p. 23.

A portrait by Robert M. Jackson appeared on the cover of Opportunity. Mr. Jackson was noted for his paintings on Negro subjects and presented a one-man show of his work in this field. He is pictured in the article.

366.   "Our Young Negro Artists." Opportunity, Vol. 1,
        January, 1923, pp. 16-18.

        Notes that exhibits of Negro artists at two public
        libraries in New York and in Boston have exposed a
        seldom recognized talent. The New York exhibit showed
        works of better known Negro artists and some local
        talent. The Boston exhibit covered graphic arts and
        music. Six paintings by five artists are shown in
        the article.

367.   Owen, Chandler. "New Ideas on Art." The Messenger,
        Vol. 7, January, 1925, pp. 23-24.

        Author feels that the function of art is to emphasize
        by exaggeration. He talks more of how the actor and
        writer can portray the beauty of ugliness of art, but
        does note how the anti-slavery artist pictured slavery
        in hideous horror. The more ugly the art, the more
        effective it was in arousing opposition to slavery.

368.   "Paintings by Negro Artists Exhibited at Corcoran
        Art Gallery." Opportunity, Vol. 17, May, 1939, p. 151.

        At the Sixteenth Biennial Exhibition of Contemporary
        Oil Paintings at the Corcoran Gallery of Art in Wash-
        ington, DC included a painting by Lois Mailou Jones
        which she did in France. A group of paintings also
        done by her in France was exhibited at the Morton Vose
        Galleries in Boston.

369.   "Painting It Like it Is: The Ghetto." The Negro Di-
        gest, Vol. 16, August, 1967, pp. 90-92.

        Frederick Campbell has captured on canvas the distinc-
        tive mood and human expression which is characteristic
        of life in the Black ghetto. Mr. Campbell studied at
        the Hussian School of Art and had his work exhibited
        at Hampton Institute. Four of his paintings and a
        picture of the artist are featured.

370.   "Paintings by Young Artist Puzzles Fairgoers." Jet,
        Vol. 36, September 11, 1969, p. 15.

        Steven A. Williams had his ten painting series,
        "Project Ghetto," on display at the Illinois State
        Fair. One in particular, showing children sleeping
        with rats puzzled fairgoers. He also paints contem-
        porary famous people.

371.   Parker, Patricia. "Two Centuries of Black American
        Art." Black Collegian, Vol. 8, September/October,
        1977, pp. 50-51.

        A major art exhibit, "Two Centuries of Black American
        Art," toured ten cities between September 30, 1976 and

(Parker, Patricia)

September 5, 1977. The exhibit is a comprehensive historical survey of the achievements of Black artists in America. Article shows six of the paintings included in the exhibit.

372. Parks, James D. "An Experiment in Painting the Local Scene." Design, Vol. 47, February, 1946, pp. 10-12.

This head of the Art Department at Lincoln University, Missouri trained his art classes from the academic way to regionalism in order to find a more enjoyable approach to painting. Regionalism limits painting to scenes with which the artist is most familiar and painting them in a highly personal manner. Three of the regionalistic paintings are shown.

373. "Part-Time Ambassador." Ebony, Vol. 14, January, 1959, pp. 69-71.

Facing prejudice in Japan when he married a Japanese, Airman Earle E. Hines decided to stand his ground. The painter opened an art school for the children. Classes were free. The attitude of the neighbors soon changed. Pictures of Airman Hines at work with his Japanese children are shown.

374. "Passing Shows." Art News, Vol. 42, November 15-30, 1943, p. 22.

Negative review of an exhibition of Negro painters from Hampton Institute at the Museum of Modern Art. The reviewer felt that only one painting had the color, dignity, and sincerity which he felt was the national heritage of the Negro and that the exhibition was the "work of heavy-handed teachers dealing with over-plastic material."

375. "Paul Lewis Clemens." Magazine of Art, Vol. 31, November, 1938, pp. 655-656.

Mr. Clemens' first solo art show at the Maynard Walker Gallery was a huge success. In the National Exhibition sponsored by the Municipal Art Committee for 1937, he had a canvas of a side show barker and Negro entertainers. One of his paintings are shown.

376. "Phillip Mason: An Artistic Bombshell." Sepia, Vol. 17, October, 1968, pp. 20-21.

Phillip L. Mason works are concerned with the positive images, the beauty of Blackness. He was awarded the Mabel Rubin Memorial Award for his painting of Odetta, and has had his works exhibited at San Joaquin Pioneer Museum. The Oakland Art Museum had one of his paintings in their permanent collection and was listed in the Archives of American Art. In addition to painting, he is a furniture designer, writer, and a fashion designer. Three of his paintings are shown and a picture of him is included.

377.   "Pictures from Sand." Sepia, Vol. 16, February, 1967, pp. 42-44.

The one hundred year old art form, "Tapis de Sable," or sand carpets can be fixed to a surface and framed. A new adhesive process can preserve the paintings for future generations. Four paintings are shown plus pictures of artists at work.

378.   Pierce, Ponchitta. "Black Art in America." Readers Digest, Vol. 112, June, 1978, pp. 176-185.

Every since colonial times, Blacks have been creating an artistic heritage. It was not until the 1920s that the Harlem Renaissance renewed a sense of identity and pride that Black artists began focusing on Black themes. Twenty-seven art pieces are shown by several artists. A historical overview of Black artistic achievement is given also.

379.   Pierre-Noel, Lois Jones. "American Negro Art in Progress." Negro History Bulletin, Vol. 30, October, 1967, pp. 6-9.

The progress of Negro artists can be recognized by their inclusion in public exhibitions. Notes the influence of African sculpture, ritualistic masks, carvings, pottery, and craft weaving. The two major periods in Negro art were the Negro Renaissance and the New Negro Movement. Many prominent Negro artists are discussed. Four paintings and one sculpture piece are shown. Also historical overview of the Negro in Art.

380.   "Poetry and Painting." Crisis, Vol. 34, May, 1927, p. 84.

Short note and picture of Hale Woodruff who received the second prize for drawing in the Crisis contest in 1926.

381.   "Poison Pen Art." Ebony, Vol. 7, July, 1952, pp. 59-61.

Brumsic Brandon, a Negro GI in Germany, developed a new cartoon technique. It was a continuous one-line drawing style. Calling them poison pen drawings, Mr. Brandon explained that he used his art to jibe the everyday foibles of the typical American. A picture of Mr. Brandon and some of his cartoons he drew for

Ebony are included.

382.   "Politics." Artforum, Vol. 9, May, 1971, p. 12.

A group of African-American artists wrote to protest
the exhibit at the Whitney Museum which they felt
neglected to include works by Black artists thus
minimizing the value of their works. They felt that
the museum has done no indepth historical research
into the quality of African-American art.

383.   Porter, Hattie. "Response to the Journal of the National Conference of Artists." Phase II, Vol. I,
Spring, 1970, p. 4.

The journal described The National Conference of Artists as the "first and only organization devoted to
the development of art among Negroes." Ms. Porter
did criticize the comment by James Parks who said that
Black art has no particular dominant style or direction.

384.   "Prairie State College." Art Journal, Vol. 31, Spring,
1972, p. 330.

The Art Department started a visiting artist series.
The first speaker was Richard Hart, CAA Board Member
and a faculty member at St. Louis Junior College
District. He spoke on "The Young Black Artist in
America."

385.   "Princeton Group Arts." Crisis, Vol. 58, January,
1951, pp. 19-22.

This group worked with children and adults, regardless
of color or creed, to give them professional instruc-
tion in the arts for a minimal fee. Classes in drawing, painting, ceramics, sculpture, singing, dancing,
and dramatics were offered. This group was known to
have struck a blow to segregation in Princeton by
admitting all races; and the author of this article
wished to remain anonymous.

386.   "Prints by Margaret G. Burroughs." Freedomways, Vol.
2, Summer, 1962, pp. 293-297.

A series of black and white prints are shown. They
include such people as Sojourner Truth and Crispus
Attucks and the scenic views depict a playground and
people riding on a bus.

387.   "Protest Art Takes to the Streets." Sepia, Vol. 27,
January, 1978, pp. 39-46.

Throughout the country protest artists were painting
their messages on the sides of public buildings. One
such artist is Floyd Sapp. Seventeen examples from

New York to San Francisco and even one on a barn in
Wisconsin are shown. This photo essay was done by
Franklin Peterson.

388.   "Questionnaire." Crisis, Vol. 31, February, 1926,
        p. 165.

        Crisis asked several artists to answer certain ques-
        tions concerning the Negro in art which was to be
        published at a later date. Those questions pertaining
        directly to painting were: can an author be criti-
        cized for painting the works or the best characters
        of a group, and what can Blacks do when they are
        continually painted at their worst and be judged by
        the public as they are painted?

389.   "Racial Strength." Time, Vol. 57, April 9, 1951,
        p. 89.

        Article on the Tenth Annual Exhibition of Negro Paint-
        ing and Sculpture at Atlanta University. Eighty-nine
        artists from seventeen states participated. Notes
        some of the winners and pieces of winning sculpture
        are shown. One patron felt the show had an "almost
        frightening racial strength and feeling."

390.   "Raise Scholarship Funds Selling Art." Jet, Vol. 39,
        January 28, 1971, p. 47.

        A group called Color Rappers at the Northern Illinois
        University in DeKalb were selling posters and student
        designed stationery to raise scholarship funds for
        Black students to come to the university. Over one
        hundred Black shops across the nation had agreed to
        sell the posters and stationery.

391.   Randall, Dudley. "A Report on the Black Arts Conven-
        tion." Negro Digest, Vol. 15, August, 1966, pp. 54-
        58.

        The First Black Arts Convention was held in Detroit,
        June 24 through 26. There were workshops on litera-
        ture, music, art, drama, education, religion, history,
        and politics.

392.   _____. "The Second Annual Black Arts Convention."
        Negro Digest, Vol. 17, November, 1967, pp. 42-48.

        This convention dealt with all types of art. In one
        session, Charles Enoch felt that art must serve the
        purpose of the movement, while Henri King felt that
        the Black artist must create things new and dynamic.
        He also felt that Black artists had not created their
        own art form. Harold Neal felt that Black artists
        must stop being a specialist and was irritated that no
        Black artist had responded to such tragedies as the

killing of Medgar Evers or the bombing of four Black girls in Birmingham.

393.   Ratcliff, Carter. "New York Letter." Art International, Vol. 14, May 20, 1970, p.78.

The sculpture of Barbara Chase-Riboud shown at the Bertha Schaefer Gallery were highly polished hand crumpled metal. Sometimes thick braids and ropes of silk were attached to the metal.

394.   "Raymond Saunders." Arts Magazine, Vol. 43, February, 1969, p. 66.

Mr. Saunders' work is hard to categorize. He superimposes hard-edged shapes over some of his lyric abstractions. The real life drama of his works can be felt beneath the surface.

395.   Reed, Ishmael. "Ending the Western Established Church of Art." Essence, Vol. 1, January, 1971, p. 15.

Mr. Reed discusses the priorities of national, state, and local foundations and their discrimination against Black artists. Notes that Black painters became so disgusted with the racist policies of tax supported museums that they turned to sabotage exhibits which contain no Third World artists. Also analysis of the role of foundations in supporting Black artists.

396.   _____. "From Wood Carving to Bronze: A Conversation with Doyle Forman." Essence, Vol. 1, Spring, 1972, pp. 62-63.

Mr. Reed asked Mr. Foreman why he uses wood to convey his art, his opinion of art critics, and how he came to do bronze casting. Mr. Doyle says his art comes from the Black experience. Two of his works and a picture of him are shown.

397.   "Reviews and Previews - Avel de Knight." Art News, Vol. 67, November, 1968, p. 13.

An exhibit at the Larcadn Art Gallery show Neo-Romantic gouaches and oils on paper which float vast, banded horizons over a silent land and shrouded figures.

398.   "Reviews and Previews." Art News, Vol. 69, March, 1970, p. 12.

Barbara Chase-Riboud held her first one-woman show in New York at the Bertha Schaefer Gallery. She showed four mysterious, moving bronzes entitled, "Four Monuments to Malcolm X." The curious combination of bronze and bronze-colored wood and silk rope and thread

coils create a humanizing recipe of strength and vul-
nerability.

399.   "Reviews and Previews - Charles White." Art News,
Vol. 69, April, 1970, p. 76.

Mr. White found a series of Civil War posters advertising slaves which inspired him to do a series of
brown and white drawings of slaves priced as in the
poster.

400.   "Reviews and Previews - Henry Ossawa Tanner." Art
News, Vol. 67, September, 1968, p. 71.

First Black artist to become a member of the National
Academy of Design, Mr. Tanner's show at the Grand
Central Art Gallery was of newly discovered works
found in Paris.

401.   "Reviews and Previews - Thomas Sills." Art News,
Vol. 69, March, 1970, p. 67.

This well known abstract-expressionist is distinguished by his broad, irregular canals of color and
stroke, plus a full-bodied inelegant sense of design
and color.

402.   "Reviews and Previews - Vincent Smith." Art News,
Vol. 67, September, 1968, pp. 14, 17.

Mr. Smith's themes depict the violence and pain of
now---Martin Luther King's funeral, riots, Viet-Nam,
ghetto life, and poverty. They are done in oils,
water colors, and bloodily technicolor photomontages.

403.   Rustin, Bayard. "The Role of the Artist in The Freedom Struggle." Crisis, Vol. 77, August/September,
1970, pp. 260-263.

Speech delivered by Mr. Rustin in presenting the Fif-
ty-fifth Spingarn Medal to Jacob Lawrence for his artistic contributions. Mr. Rustin said that artists
are essential members of the freedom struggle. The
artist reflects the ways in which our people live.
"The Negro artist is the ultimate and the only unfet-
tered clear voice of the aspiration of the Black community. The Black artists' role is to reveal to all
the human core of the human experience as seen through
the Black experience." Article on the role of the
Black artist.

404.   "Sanford and His World of Art." Negro Digest, Vol.
12, June, 1963, pp. 40-43, 53.

A profile of Walter Sanford, a realist painter. He
was working on a series of portraits of real and ima-

ginary figures which were portraits - indepth, baring
the subjects' souls. He had very little formal art
education and until 1945 his style was generally
expressionist, then a switch to abstract-expressionism
and in 1963, a return to realism. An appraisal of his
work is given by Aral who was a former art critic.
Aral notes that Sanford's work had a unique style. He
felt that Sanford was at ease in many fields of artistic expression. He talked of Sanford's painting,
"The Philosopher," (pictured) and notes that this work
revealed clearly Sanford's dynamic strength.

405. Scarbrough, W. S. "Henry Ossawa Tanner." Southern
      Workman, Vol. 31, December, 1902, pp. 661-670.

After teaching at a southern college, Mr. Tanner went
to Paris in 1891 to study under Jean Paul Laurens at
the Julian School of Art. He discusses the fine techniques of many of his works, especially the ones with
religious themes. Tanner chose France as his home because of its lack of racial prejudice. His works depicting race subjects were thought to counterbalance
the treatment of the race by other artists as grotesque and humorous. A picture of Mr. Tanner and four of
his works are shown.

406. Schjeldaht, Peter. "New York Letter." Art Interna-
      tional, Vol. 13, October, 1969, pp. 74-79.

One of the exhibits covered in this article is "Harlem
On My Mind," at the Metropolitan Museum of Modern Art.
He notes the demand for more showings of Black artists'
works and how some galleries were handling this demand.
The Lee Nordness Galleries Exhibit on Afro-American
Artists Since 1950 which gathered works throughout
the country but left out African forms. The Studio
Museum of Harlem's Exhibit on Harlem Artists Since
1969 showed the works of fifty-three local artists.
Brooklyn College dedicated an art exhibit on the works
of the late Bob Thompson and other promising artists.
Three works, one by each, Al Hollingsworth, Richard
Hunt, and Bob Thompson, are shown.

407. Schlick, Robert. "Theatre and the Arts." Crisis,
      Vol. 39, March, 1932, p. 90.

Tells of the exhibit by Richmond Barthe's sculpture and
an exhibit of prints by James Lesesne Wells. Short
paragraph on the astounding career of Mr. Barthe and
the many recognitions his sculpture has received. Mr.
Wells' exhibit at the Delphia Studio is characterized
as racial, original, and virile. He used many subject
matters: heads, buildings, workers, etc. Article on

(Schlick, Robert)

the artists with some critical analysis of Mr. Wells' works.

408.   Schuyler, George S. "Art and the Color Bar." Messenger, Vol. 6, July, 1924, p. 232.

Discussion with O. Richard Reid, portrait painter, on
how color prejudice hampered the Negro artist. Mr.
Reid felt that with knowledge, skill, and determina-
tion, the Negro could overcome the pressures of race
prejudice. He also discussed how he was able to paint
the portraits of many prominent people. A picture of
Mr. Reid and one of his portraits are shown.

409.   _____. "The Negro-Art Hokum." Nation, Vol. 122,
June, 1926, pp. 662-663.

In terms of Black literature, painting, and sculpture,
Mr. Schuyler felt that it was identical in kind with
that of White Americans showing evidence of European
influence. He felt that Blacks experience the same
social and economic forces as Whites and that contrary
to popular belief, Blacks were no different from
Whites and should not be expected to produce art and
literature dissimilar to that produced by Whites.

410.   Schwartz, Theresa. "The Political Scene." Arts Magazine, Vol. 45, April, 1971, p. 19.

Ten Black artists spoke on the panel at the Art Students' League in New York and another ten Black non-
panel members spoke. The panel discussed their lives
as artists and noted that the Black artist has never
been at home in the art community. They talked of
the difficulty in getting showings, selling works, and
their exclusion from national shows. Two Black women
also spoke of the obstacles of Black female artists.

411.   Scott, John S. "The Black Aesthetic in Life and Art."
Black Lines, Vol. 2, Fall, 1971, pp. 39-41.

This article looks at the function of the Black aesthetic in art. The author feels that this function is
to restore the consciousness, the natural goodness of
the "Black Essence," and enrich all people with the
essence of their Blackness. Art must inspire men to
reach for and grasp inner-attainment. Art is a reflection of everything and thus everything is art.
The energy of life and Art must be to defend, recreate
and enrich the Black Aesthetic for all humanity - all
the Black spawns.

412.   "Seeing the Light." Jet, Vol. 19, March 30, 1961,
p. 47.

Alvin C. Hollingsworth developed "painting in light" which was hailed as a new dimension in fine arts. A picture of him talking with the owner of Ward Eggelston Gallery is shown.

413. "Seer of Beauty." Crisis, Vol. 15, January, 1918, p. 128.

Notes the death of Richard Brown at the age of 24. He was helped by the artist George deForest Brush and the NAACP. On a trip South to capture the beauty of the landscape there, Mr. Brown caught pneumonia in Oklahoma and died.

414. "Selma Burke." Ebony, Vol. 2, March, 1947, pp. 32-35.

Seldom working on impulse, Selma Burke tackled a sub- ject only after long and thoughtful planning. She opened an art school and her work had little racial flavor with her most prized works being, "Salome," "Lafayette," and the statute of Franklin D. Roosevelt. She had won the contest to do the statute but Roose- velt died before the statute was completed but she fin- ished it and it hangs in the Hall of Records in Wash- ington, DC. There are several pictures of Ms. Burke at work and with art students.

415. "Sermon in Oils." Jet, Vol. 19, February 9, 1961, p. 45.

Ben Flowers completed a twelve month project of paint- ing a 22 x 12 1/2 feet oil painting of "The Last Sup- per" for Mercy Hospital in Ohio. A picture of him with the painting is shown.

416. Shapiro, David. "652 Broadway." Art News, Vol. 70, April, 1971, pp. 52, 85-86.

Talks about the works of William T. Williams who has the eleventh floor at 652 Broadway. His "Overkill" show has a formal and psycho-social allegory. His paintings are filled with almost harmonal activity. An overview of some of his works is given and two of his works are shown.

417. "Shoe Polish Painter." Ebony, Vol. 3, August, 1948, p. 55.

Bootblack James Howard paints portraits and landscapes with shoe polish. He was also an actor and playwright. He often collected autographs of famous people whose shoes he shined in exchange for one of his paintings.

418. "Show Stopper." Jet, Vol. 18, June 23, 1960, p. 52.

Artist Eric Anderson examines one of the paintings on

display at Fifty-Seventh Street Art Fair in Chicago.

419.   "Shower Curtain Artists." Ebony, Vol. 8, February, 1953, pp. 84-87.

An interracial group of artists were employed by Styletone, Inc. to hand paint shower curtains. The company was started in 1946. They turn out the shower curtains on a mass-production basis. Half of the employees are Negroes and one-tenth are handicapped. One big event for the company employees was an annual art show of paintings and sculptures. Several pictures of the artists at work are shown.

420.   Siegel, Jeanne. "Why Spiral." Art News, Vol. 65, September, 1966, p. 48.

Fourteen artists in New York discuss the problems facing the Black artists today. Among the artists were: Romare Bearden, Charles Alston, Hale Woodruff, James Yeargans, Alvin Hollingsworth, etc. Sixteen works by various artists are shown.

421.   Skerett, Jr., Joseph T. "Edward M. Bannister, Afro-American Painter (1828-1901)." Negro History Bulletin, Vol. 41, May/June, 1978, p. 829.

This neglected artist works are now becoming famous. Like other Nineteenth Century Black figures, his life and works are filled with inaccuracies. One of his works, "Under The Oaks," (now lost) was awarded the bronze medal at the Centennial Exposition in 1876. He helped organize the Providence Art Club.

422.   Smith, Hughie-Lee. "The Negro Artist in America Today." Negro History Bulletin, Vol. 27, February, 1964, pp. 111-112.

Notes the many hardships and discriminations experienced by early Black artists, his lack of patronage by Blacks forcing him to rely on White patrons, and limiting the kind of subject matter he can exploit. Author feels that the Black middle class had to be reorientated to spearhead a renaissance of interest into the works of Black artists and make it possible for them to reflect our social revolution.

423.   Smith, Lucy E. "Some American Painters in Paris." American Magazine of Art, Vol. 18, March, 1927, pp. 134-136.

One Black artist is featured in this article on American painters in Paris. Henry O. Tanner's work, "Raising of Lazarus," was cited as having originality of idea and deep feeling. Notes the masterly grouping and facial expression and how the colors suit the

(Smith, Lucy E.)

supernatural character of the scene.

424. "Spring Annuals." Art News, Vol. 44, April 15-30,
     1945, pp. 8-9.

     Notes the Fourth Annual Exhibition of the works of
     Negro artists at Atlanta University. Lists the win-
     ners and honorable mentions.

425. Steinbach, Sophia. "Harlem Goes In for Art." Op-
     portunity, Vol. 14, April, 1936, pp. 114-116.

     The Federal Art Project of the WPA established a free
     art class in Harlem in 1934. Augusta Savage provided
     the studio space for classes which was to bring out
     creative abilities in each child. Adult classes were
     held along with discussion groups. Requests for the
     art works of the children were requested for exhibits
     in other states. Pictures of the students in their
     classes are shown.

426. "Studio Watts Learning Center for the Arts." Art
     Journal, Vol. 29, Fall, 1969, p. 35.

     The Third Annual Watts Chalk-In was held as a way to
     bring the community together. The best chalk drawing
     won a prize. It was also used as a way the studio re-
     cruited new apprentices. A photographic exhibit was
     held later and a special exhibit on African art was
     shown so the community could see original African art.
     Article also discusses what one organization was doing
     to foster Black art.

427. "Survey." Opportunity, Vol. 6, July, 1928, p. 217.

     James Lesesne Wells whose wood cut on the cover of
     Opportunity has had works exhibited at the One Hundred
     Thirty-Fifth Branch of the New York Public Library,
     the Holtz Gallery, Anderson's Gallery, and Butler's
     Art Museum. He had previously done paintings but
     turned to wood cuts and was interested in the adapta-
     tion of wood cuts to commercial design.

428. "Survey of the Month - Art." Opportunity, Vol. 10,
     May, 1931, p. 156.

     The works of Olga Hewett, a student of fashion illu-
     stration was held at the One Hundred Thirty-Fifth
     Branch of the New York Public Library. The exhibi-
     tion was held to gain professional contacts for the
     talented lady whose work was described as artistic
     and practical.

429.   "Survey of the Month - Art." Opportunity, Vol. 9,
        October, 1931, p. 320.

        Notes the return of Negro artist Hale Woodruff to the
        United States after four years in France. His works
        were being exhibited at two art galleries in New York.

430.   Tarshis, Jerome. "San Francisco." Artforum, Vol. 9,
        October, 1970, p. 81.

        The works of five Black artists were shown at the
        Oakland Museum entitled "Black Untitled." All artists
        lived in the Bay area and none of their works had been
        previously exhibited. The five artists were: William
        Henderson, an expressionist artist whose work is shown
        in the article; Henry Rollins, a sculptor; Donald
        Coles, a painter; Leslie Price, a painter; and
        Michael Greene, depicting his box constructions.

431.   _____. "San Francisco." Art Forum, Vol. 9, Decem-
        ber, 1970, pp. 84-85.

        Notes the Third Anniversary of the Black Man's Art
        Gallery with an exhibit representing the gallery's
        twelve artists. Founded by Juba Solo (W. O. Bill
        Thomas, Jr.) because there was no place for Blacks to
        go see themselves represented in art, nor was there
        a place for Black artists to have their works shown.
        Located in a Black neighborhood, it provided cultural
        services to the whole Bay Area. Joe Overstreet's
        paintings were on display at the Berkley Art Center.
        His paintings are like shields or spiderwebs and they
        are attached to the wall and floor by ropes passed
        through grommets. His works gain added power by draw-
        ing upon the traditional art of other cultures.

432.   Taylor, Bob. "California Black Craftsmen." Phase II,
        Vol. 1, Spring, 1970.

        The first California Black Craftsmen Exhibit opened
        at Mills College Art Gallery in Oakland and would go
        on tour afterwards. It had two hundred works by
        nineteen Bay Area and Southern California craftsmen.
        Organized by E. J. Montgomery who was also responsible
        for the first regional museum show of Black paintings
        and sculpture in 1968. Included were assemblages,
        stitchery, ceramics, jewelry, and weaving.

433.   Taylor, E. A. "The American Colony of Artists in
        Paris." International Studio, Vol. 46, June, 1912,
        pp. 280-290.

        Among the artists Mr. Taylor talks about one Black is
        included. Henry O. Tanner's works depict Christian
        religion in art. He has an excellent color sense.
        One of his paintings, "The Wise and Foolish," is shown.

434.   "Theadius McCall: Impatient Young Artist." Sepia,
        Vol. 16, August, 1967, pp. 76-80.

        Beginning his art career as a teenager, Mr. McCall
        used a secret painting process to turn out a huge
        masterpiece in one and one-half hours. He opened the
        Hemis Art Gallery in Houston. His pictures show po-
        verty, social injustices, and the blues. Pictures of
        Mr. McCall at work and several of his paintings are
        shown.

435.   "Thomas Hart Benton on Art." Midwest Journal, Vol. 6,
        Fall, 1954, pp. 64-76.

        The National Conference of Teachers of Art in Negro
        Colleges held on April 29, 1954 at Lincoln University
        invited noted artist, Thomas Hart Benton. There was
        a question and answer session conducted.

436.   Thompson, W. O. "Collins and DeVillis - Two Promising
        Painters." Voice of the Negro, Vol. 2, October, 1905,
        pp. 685-691.

        Talks of the artistic talents of Samuel O. Collins and
        J. Clinton DeVillis. Mr. Collins dealt mainly with
        landscapes while Mr. DeVillis dealt with landscapes
        and the human figure. Pictures of Mr. Collins and Mr.
        DeVillis are shown plus four paintings by Collins and
        two by DeVillis.

437.   Thurman, Wallace. "Negro Artists and the Negro."
        New Republic, Vol. 52, August 31, 1927, pp. 37-39.

        Notes the renewed Black art fad, and then the sudden
        fading of excitement and how it causes Blacks to look
        at themselves with some being proud, while others be-
        came angry that works were being produced that did not
        qualify as "respectable ." The artists, Aaron Douglas
        and Richard Bruce were among those in disfavor;
        Douglas for his advanced modernism; and Bruce, for his
        interest in decadent types. Goes on to cite the more
        serious endeavors to evaluate the present and the
        future significance of this development in Black life,
        plus interpreting and utilizing those things with true
        aesthetic value.

438.   "To Encourage Negro Art." Crisis, Vol. 29, November,
        1924, p. 11.

        The Crisis cited its eagerness to discover ability
        among Blacks in literature and art. Mentions its
        covers by William Scott, Laura Wheeler, William Farrow,
        and Richard Brown, and its cartoons by Lorenzo Harris
        and Albert Smith. Both The Crisis and Opportunity
        offered prizes to Black artists in excess of one thou-
        sand dollars to further encourage artists.

439.   Toldson, Ivory L.   "Developmental Stages of Black
        Self-Discovery: Implications for Using Black Art Forms
        in Group Interaction." Journal of Negro Education,
        Vol. 44, Spring, 1975, pp. 130-137.

        Black art forms which are rooted in the folk life of
        Blacks contain images that can revive previously re-
        pressed elements of Blackness. These new art forms
        also have therapeutic value for they allow for the
        expression of effective energy. A psycho-philosophi-
        cal interpretation of Black art.

440.   "Toledo Artist Gains Note with Catchy Book Jackets."
        Jet, Vol. 20, April 27, 1961, p. 49.

        Commercial artist, Roger Crawford, gained fame for his
        novelty book jacket designs. The catchy titles in-
        cluded, "Forgery," "Self-Taught," and "Head Shrinking."
        A picture of Mr. Crawford is included.

441.   "Tom Feelings." Freedomways, Vol. 2, Spring, 1962,
        p. 160.

        A series of seven black and white pictures by noted
        artist Tom Feelings.

442.   "Two Generations of Black Artists." Art Interna-
        tional, Vol. 14, October 20, 1970, p. 74.

        California State College presented an exhibit on "Two
        Generations of Black Artists" which included works by
        Charles White, Bettye Saar, Ron Moore, and David
        Hammons. Most of the article centered on the accom-
        plishments of Mr. Hammons and one of his paintings was
        shown. Mr. Hammons was known for developing "body
        prints."

443.   "Two Negro Artists Win Awards in 'Artists for Victory'
        Exhibition." Opportunity, Vol. 21, January, 1943,
        p. 18.

        Two artists, Richmond Barthe and Jacob Lawrence, won
        awards at the "Artists for Victory Exhibition." Mr.
        Barthe won for his sculpture, "Boxer," and Mr. Law-
        rence won for his color painting, "Pool Parlor." A
        short biographical sketch on Mr. Barthe's numerous
        awards are given. Pictures of the winning art works
        from both authors are shown.

444.   "Unknown Black Artists Get Chance to Show their Work."
        Jet, Vol. 39, February 4, 1971, pp. 48-49.

        Sixty Black artists were featured in an exhibit tour-
        ing Illinois sponsored by the Illinois Arts Council.
        Entitled "Black American Artists/71," it had one
        hundred fifty works by such artists as Jacob Lawrence,

Romare Bearden, Richard Mayhew, and Sam Gilliam. The
art expressed many racial idioms. Four pictures of
various artists and their works are shown.

445. Vlach, John. "Graveyards and Afro-American Art."
Southern Exposure, Vol. 5, Summer/Fall, 1977, pp. 161-
165.

The decorations used in Black graveyards are often
different from what is found in a White graveyard.
Grave offerings can be traced to African religious
practices. Decorations vary widely but most are
pottery or pressed glass. These objects on the graves
constitute a visual environment which in the Black
tradition, embodies the world of spirits, and often
the spirits of ancestors. They are sanctified testimonies of material messages left by the living to
pacify the deceased and keep the stormy souls at rest.

446. "Wall of Respect." Ebony, Vol. 23, December, 1967,
pp. 48-50.

The side wall of a slum building in Chicago became a
mural communicating Black dignity. Such Black not-
ables as W. E. B. DuBois, LeRoi Jones, Muhammad Ali,
Nina Simone, Stokely Carmichael, Sarah Vaughan, Rap
Brown, John O. Killens, Wilt Chamberlain, and others
were among those many Black portrayed on the wall.
Members of the Organization of Black American Culture (OBAC) created the landmark which became known
as the "Wall of Respect." Several pictures of the
wall, artists at work on the wall, and the community
viewing the wall are included.

447. Ward, Francis, and Val Gray Ward. "The Black Artist-
His Role in the Struggle." Black Scholar, Vol. 2,
January, 1971, pp. 23-32.

Discusses the role of the Black artist in the Black
Liberation Movement. The authors are speaking of
all Black artists (dancers, singers, painters, com-
posers, etc.). Discusses the six roles the Black
artist will play in the future: creator, critic,
hero figure to young Blacks, activist, propagandist,
and fundraiser.

448. "Washington Art Comes Home." Our World, Vol. 6,
May, 1951, pp. 30-32.

The Black sponsored Barnett-Aden Gallery in Washington, DC opened its Eighth season with an exhibition
of twenty contemporary paintings by Black and White
artists. Several paintings are shown along with some
prominent persons who help make the gallery a success.

449. Watkins, Richard. "Jacob Lawrence." Black Enterprise, Vol. 6, December, 1975, pp. 66-68.

(Watkins, Richard)

Notes that Jacob Lawrence's works are so distinctive that many people know his works without being able to recall his name. He had works hanging in the Metropolitan Museum of Art, The Museum of Modern Art, and the Whitney Museum where he sold his first work in 1941. He had been described as "Heir to the Negro Renaissance and Child of the Depression," because he chronicles the important events of Black History.

450. "We Find this Deeply Disturbing . . ." Negro Digest, Vol. 8, June, 1966, p. 97.

This editorial criticized the First World Festival of Negro Arts. The selection of a White to represent Black people was the point of criticism. It was felt that a Black did not have the position, responsibility, capabilities, or wealth to carry out the festival. The editors felt that Black masses should have been given the chance to make the festival a success.

451. Weathers, Diane. "Artists and the 'Fine Art' of Survival." Black Enterprise, Vol. 6, December, 1975, pp. 18-24.

Looks at where Black artists stand today. Notes the help of non-profit art institutions which display the works of Black artists but they also call attention to the problem of separate facilities for Black artists and how they lose their power outside the Black community. He examines the works of Richard Hunt, Al Loving, Howardena Pindell, and Suzanne Jackson. Picture of each artist at work is shown.

452. Weaver, Alfred. "Black is Not a Color." Art and Artist, Vol. 4, May, 1966, pp. 14-17.

The author raises questions concerning Black art. Mr. Weaver felt that there is such a thing as Black art but Black artists must meet every single kind of competition in the open market. He notes the attitudes of some major Black artists: Charles Alston, Jacob Lawrence, Hughie Lee-Smith, etc. Seven paintings by several Black artists are shown. An editorial note is included stating that Dr. Weaver's opinions are his own.

453. Wesley, Charles H. "Henry O. Tanner, The Artist - An Appreciation." Howard University Record, Vol. 14, April, 1920, pp. 299-306.

Historical biography on the career, work, and manner in which his work was received by the critical art world, and how he was inspired to paint. By 1901, one

(Wesley, Charles H.)

of his paintings had received a medal. Much of his career was spent overseas where he gained critical acclaim.

454.   Wilkins, Roy. "Sculptor by Accident." Crisis, Vol. 41, October, 1934, p. 307.

Beginning his art career as a painter, Richmond Barthe later tried to sculptor and found that this was where his talents lay. He had his first one-man show in 1930 where he exhibited forty pieces of art work at the Woman's City Club in Chicago. He won many awards. His first show in New York was in 1931 at the Caz-Delbo Galleries. He received a Rosenwald Scholarship in 1931. Some of his works are in the Whitney Museum, the Gary Indiana Childrens' Home, and Haiti used his bust of Toussaint L'Overture as a frontispiece for a new book on L'Overture.

455.   "William A. Farrow - Etcher." Opportunity, Vol. 7, June, 1929, p. 188.

First receiving recognition in 1923 when one of his water colors hung at the International Water Color Exhibition, Mr. Farrow won prizes in 1928 and 1929 for his etchings. Two of his etchings are shown in this short but informative article on Mr. Farrow.

456.   Williams, Fannie Barrier. "Refining Influence of Art." Voice of the Negro, Vol. 3, March, 1906, pp. 211-214.

Notes the work of a Chicago woman's club and the Central Art Association in developing a circulating art collection for schools and homes to foster art appreciation.

457.   Williams, Milton. "America's Top Black Artist." Sepia, Vol. 23, August, 1974, pp. 75-78.

Notes the nationwide series of museum shows of Jacob Lawrence's works sponsored by IBM. It opened at the Whitney Museum and had one hundred sixty-three art works. Encouraged by Charles Alston, Lawrence went on to win a scholarship to the American Artists' School. He has also received Rosenwald Fellowships. A biographical sketch of Mr. Lawrence is given. His works have been criticized as being passe and out-dated, but his works reflect the Black experience and he has done a series of paintings on such people as Frederick Douglass and Harriet Tubman. A picture of Mr. Lawrence and four of his paintings are shown.

458.   Williams, Randy. "The Black Artist as Activist."
        Black Creation, Vol. 3, Winter, 1972, pp. 42-45.

        Author feels that for a complete and functional sur-
        vival of Black art there must be support of the philo-
        sophy of Black Activist-Artist and the Black activists
        must have their own institutions. The activist-artist
        must effect evolution and revolution and unite the two
        ideas so Blacks can understand them. The function of
        revolutionary art is to maintain the aspirations and
        spirit of the Black public. Three works are shown.
        This article is also an example of the ideas of Black
        artists during the early 1970s.

459.   Willig, Nancy Tobin. "Anger and Heritage." Art News,
        Vol. 73, December, 1974, pp. 62-63.

        Directions in Afro-American Art was on exhibit at Cor-
        nell University's Herbert Johnson Museum. It took two
        years to organize with a grant from the National Endow-
        ment of the Arts. Twenty-eight artists were shown.
        The catalogue introduction notes the four basic direc-
        tions in Afro-American art: social protest, rediscovery
        of the African/Caribbean heritage, depiction of the
        Black experience in America, and the Black consciousness
        in the mainstream of modern art.

460.   Winslow Vernon. "Negro Art and the Depression." Op-
        portunity, Vol. 19, February, 1941, pp. 40-42, 62-63.

        Had it not been for the NYA and WPA during the depres-
        sion, Negro artists would have all but vanished. A new
        art agency, the Community Art Center and other centers
        dedicated its program of strengthening of art through
        industry. The artist not only reached a greater market
        but also saw his work in relationship to use of other
        contemporary expression.

461.   _____. "Making the Negroes' Art Practicable." Op-
        portunity, Vol. 18, September, 1940, pp. 262-263, 277-
        278.

        Cites the need for Black colleges to broaden their ex-
        tracurricular activities. Notes the need for art clas-
        ses to include community handicrafts or the art of de-
        signing useful articles from the natural resources of
        the community. Also a critical analysis of the areas
        that need to be updated in art training.

462.   Wolseley, Roland E. "The Black Press and Black Art."
        Encore, Vol. 4, May 19, 1975, p. 32.

        Mr. Wolseley speaks of the allegations of Benny Andrews
        and Art Forum editor, John Coplans that Black publica-
        tions ignore Black artists. He takes exception to this
        and states that there is not enough coverage of

(Wolseley, Roland E.)

sculpture and painting and criticisms of those art
forms but there is much coverage of music, dance,
photographs, film, and popular arts. Cites the lack
of a desire by the news audience for this type of art
criticism, the fact that art draws little advertising
revenue and the need for more art appreciation courses
to acquaint the public more with art. When art becomes
newsworthy the media will devote more time to it.

463.   Woodruff, Hale. "My Meeting with Henry O. Tanner."
        Crisis, Vol. 77, January, 1970, pp. 6-12.

        Mr. Woodruff relates his first meeting with Henry O.
        Tanner some forty-two years ago in Paris. The conver-
        sation revealed the percepts which guided Mr. Tanner
        to form his artistic principles. Two paintings done
        by Mr. Tanner, one painting of Mr. Tanner done by
        Thomas Eakin, and a picture of Mr. Woodruff are in-
        cluded. Mr. Woodruff has recently retired as Profes-
        sor of Art at New York University.

464.   _____. "Negro Artists Hold Fourth Annual in At-
        lanta." Art Digest, Vol. 19, April, 15, 1945, p. 10.

        Ninety-one pieces were on display at the Fourth Annual
        Exhibition of Art by Negroes at Atlanta University.
        The works represented a divergence of subjects, styles,
        and artistic viewpoints. Almost devoid of racial
        qualities, it was a cross-section of art by American
        Negroes. One thousand four hundred dollars in prizes
        were given to the artists. The winning landscape,
        "Winter Sports," by Henry Bannard is shown.

5
DISSERTATIONS

465. Coleman, Floyd Willis. "Persistence and Discontunity of Traditional African Perception in Afro-American Art." Unpublished Ph.D. Dissertation, University of Georgia, 1975.

This is a study of African-influenced art in the United States. The writer argues that long enduration to the traditional African environment combined with a religious outlook informed by the traditional West African World view, contributed strongly to the retention of Africanism in the art of Afro-Americans. He concludes that traditional African modes of perception are far more extensive in Afro-American art than has been commonly realized and that this persistent influence should be considered in any critical estimate of works by Afro-American artists in the United States.

466. DePillars, Murry Norman. "African-American Artists and Art Students: A Morphological Study in the Urban Black Aesthetic." Unpublished Ph.D. Dissertation, Pennsylvania State University, 1976.

The writer investigates five areas: (1) the Black artists' and art students' assessment of their role in their community; (2) the explicit and/or implicit attitudes as perceived by the visual art participants of art instructors and art critics to works of art denoting racial consciousness; (3) the attitudes of community residents to works of art that denote racial consciousness; (4) the perceived stresses that occur when those artists or art students participating in the study produced works of art that denote racial consciousness in the community; and (5) to record and analyze the participants' notions of Black aesthetic. The writer also discusses the socio-historical development of Black people, especially the Black artist.

467. Gordan, Allan Moran. "Cultural Dualism on Themes of

(Gordan, Allan Moran)

Certain Afro-American Artists." Unpublished Ph.D.
Dissertation, Ohio State University, 1969.

The writer contends that there is a significant cor-
relation between the content of the art produced by
the Black artist and the existent social, political,
and economic status of the Afro-Americans; consequently, there is an emphasis on themes of aliena-
tion which reflects the Afro-Americans' marginal
status. Dr. Gordon concludes that as the Black
American artist, as an "outsider," continues to reveal
important insights into American values and life, he
will subsequently reflect other ways of viewing the
condition of man.

468.   Holmes, Oakley Norman. "Black Artists in America:
An Introduction to Seven Internationally Recognized
Black Visual Artists." Unpublished Ed.D. Dissertation,
Teachers College, Columbus University, 1973.

The seven artists discussed are Romare Bearden, Elton
Fax, Selma Burke, Palmer Hayden, Richard Mayhew,
Thomas Sills, and Charles White. The writer surmises
that Black artists express themselves in a wide range
of styles using every medium possible, but art works
produced by Afro-Americans led to an identification
of the artists with their works. This has resulted in
an exclusion of their work from classification and
from recognition. Afro-American artists, like other
artists, originally wanted to be recognized on their
individual merit, but this did not happen. Dr. Holmes
concludes that his study represents only the beginning
of a massive amount of work that needs to be done before the available teaching materials on the subject
Afro-American art approximates the proportion of work
being produced by the artists themselves.

469.   Manier, Andrew Cecil, Jr. "Past and Present American
Black Painters' and Sculptors' Contributions to
American Culture from 1919 to the Present." Unpublished Ed.D. Dissertation, Wayne State University,
1975.

The author contends that there were many outstanding
Black painters and sculptors in America from 1619 to
present and that many of these great names are unknown
to most Americans. Dr. Manier argues that the subject
of the Black artists and sculptors is more often
American that simply Black and that they were generally,
at least prior to 1900, reflectors of the total American culture stream. He concludes that in recent years
Black artists and sculptors have been concerned with
Blackness and culture pluralism in their works.

470. Meo, Yvonne Cole. "Survey on Traditional Arts of West
      Africa and Contemporary Black American Art: A Study
      of Symbolic Parallels and Cultural Transfer." Unpub-
      lished Ph.D. Dissertation, Union Graduate School -
      West, 1977.

      The author contends that indigenous West African art
      influenced Black American art through symbolism. Dr.
      Meo discusses the social psychological evolution of
      Black American art. The transferral to and the sur-
      vival of these symbols in the Black American culture
      as observed in the work produced by Black artists
      interviewed is discussed and illustrated.

471. Ransaw, Lee Andrew. "Black Mural Art and its Repre-
      sentation of the Black Community." Unpublished Ed.D.
      Dissertation, Illinois State University, 1973.

      The work describes and interprets four outdoor murals
      by Black artists. These brought about community pride,
      beauty, and dignity in the Black community. The
      writer concludes that the murals contribute to his-
      torical and current knowledge about the Black com-
      munity and was found that the murals portrayed func-
      tional and dysfunctional social institutions. Alter-
      native institutions, created and controlled by Blacks,
      are depicted as being the most acceptable for the
      Black community.

472. Simon, Walter Augustus. "Henry O. Tanner - A Study of
      the Development of an American Negro Artist: 1859 -
      1937." Unpublished Ed.D. Dissertation, New York Uni-
      versity, 1960.

      This work is concerned with the evolution of Tanner,
      who decided upon a career in art two decades after the
      Civil War when the social and economic conditions of
      the Black man in American society was at its nadir.
      The writer argues that in the narration of the life
      of Henry O. Tanner, a story unfolds that convincingly
      establishes without any element of doubt, that a
      Black venturing into a field of endeavor rarely con-
      sidered by Blacks before him, did succeed and with
      great honor.

473. Spellman, Robert Clarence. "A Comparative Analysis
      of the Characteristics of Works and Aesthetic Philo-
      sophies of Selected Contemporary Mainstream and Black-
      stream Afro-American Artists." Unpublished Ph.D. Dis-
      sertation, New York University, 1973.

      This study consists of fourteen Afro-American artists
      selected from twenty-two exhibitions of works speci-
      fically created by Black artists. These included
      Alma Thomas, David Driskell, Sam Gilliam, Alvin Loving,
      Tom Lloyd, Richard Hunt, Richard Mayhew, and Hale Wood-

(Spellman, Robert Clarence)

ruff, classified mainstream Afro-American artists;
Elizabeth Catlett, Benny Andrews, Bill Howell, Ben
Jones, Dana Chandler, and Rosalind Jefferes were
classified as Blackstream Afro-American artists. The
writer compares the aesthetic philosophies of artists
with respect to the existence or non-existence of a
Black aesthetic in the visual arts. The author concludes that mainstream artists emphasize individuality
and originality while the Blackstream artists emphasize
a sense of group solidarity, a collective artistic
unity, or a shared Black experience.

474. Williams, Althea Bulls. "The Social Mileau and the
      Black Artist in America - 1900 - 1940." Unpublished
      Ph.D. Dissertation, University of Oregon, 1972.

      This work discusses the effect of social conditions,
      as they have existed in America, and their influence
      on Black artists engaged in the visual arts between
      1900 and 1970. The author gives an overview of the
      period from 1865 - 1900. Dr. Williams concludes that
      the anonymity of the Black artists can be attributed
      to their separation from the Black masses, and to the
      tenuous position they have held on the periphery of
      the dominant culture. Their position reflects not
      only American society's lack of commitment to the arts,
      but it further reflects the dominant culture's ascrip-
      tion of Black Americans to a lower class social status.

475. Williams, Hobie L. "The Impact of the Atlanta Univer-
      sity Exhibition of Black Artists (1942 - 1969) on
      Black and Non-Black People." Unpublished Ed.D. Dis-
      sertation, University of Pittsburgh, 1973.

      The writer contends that the Atlanta University Exhi-
      bition emancipated the Black artists from the prohi-
      bitions of a racist society by allowing many of them a
      chance to participate in an exhibition at least once a
      year. He feels that the Atlanta University Exhibi-
      tion promoted a better understanding of art education,
      art history, the visual arts, and art appreciation of
      the visual expressions of the Black artists for Black
      and White people. Dr. Williams concludes that the ex-
      hibition proved that there was no difference in the
      selection of subjects between the Black artist and
      other American artists between 1942 and 1969 except
      for the choice of subjects depicting racism as chosen
      by some Black artists.

476. Young, Walter Byron. "Black American Painters and the
      Civil Rights Movement: A Study of Relationships,
      1955 - 1970." Unpublished Ed.D. Dissertation, Pennsyl-
      vania State University, 1972.

(Young, Walter Byron)

The writer argues that the Black painters are of a
general opinion that the Civil Rights Movement provided
the impetus for a renewal of interest in utilizing
more Black imagery in their own works of arts. Black
painters indicated a tendency to perfer non-objective
styles over descriptive ones, and at the same time,
feel that this mode of painting can be related to condition that makes up the uniqueness of the Black experience in America. Dr. Young concludes that the
material contained in his study may inspire creative
imagery and usuage of minority-oriented visual aids as
sources for identity enforcement and sustaining intel-
lectual interest.

6
BLACK ARTWORKS AT THE NATIONAL ARCHIVES

BLACK ART WORKS AT THE NATIONAL ARCHIVES*

1. Richmond Barthé, Sculptor (1901 -   )
    Benga
    Detail of Dance
    Gypsy Rose Lee
    Jesus Christ
    Jimmie
    Rug Cutters
    Stevedore
    Booker T. Washington

2. Romare Bearden, Painter (1912 -   )
    After Church

3. Claude Clarke, Painter (1914 -   )
    Station House
    Noon

4. Charles Davis, Painter (1912 -   )
    Tycoon Toys

5. Arthur Diggs, Painter (1888 -   )
    De Lawd and Noah

6. Aaron Douglas, Painter (1899 -   )
    Power Plant, Harlem

*In 1967 the Harmon Foundation donated some
of its records to the National Archives and
Records Service. This donation consisted of
photographic copies of art works by Blacks.
Most of the art works were exhibited during
the years 1928 - 1945.

7.   Robert S. Duncanson, Painter
      Blue Hole, Little Miami River

8.   John W. Hardrick, Painter (1891 -   )
      Two Boys Fishing

9.   Edwin A. Harleston, Painter (1882 - 1931)
      Portrait of Aaron Douglas
      The Old Servant

10.   Palmer Hayden, Painter (1893 -   )
      Baptizin' Day
      Midsummer Night in Harlem
      When Tricky Sam Shot Father Lamb
      Ballad of John Henry
      When John Was a Baby
      Where'd You Git Them High Top Shoes
      Died Wid His Hammer in His Hand

11.   Malvin Gray Johnson, Painter (1896 - 1934)
      Negro Masks
      Come Up Sometime
      Self Portrait
      Thinnin' Corn

12.   William H. Johnson, Painter (1902 -   )
      Landscape
      Sonny
      Landscape With Sun Setting
      Self Portrait
      Portrait

13.   Joshua Johnston, Painter (1765 - 1830)
      The McCormick Family

14.   Lois Mailou Jones, Painter (1906 -   )
      Ascent of Ethiopia
      Negro Youth
      Three Old Companions

15.   Jacob Lawrence, Painter (1917 -   )
      Migration of the Negro Series:
        Seven Paintings
      1. During World War I, there was a great
          migration North by Southern Negroes.
      2. Negroes were leaving by the hundreds
          to go North and enter Northern in-
          dustry.
      3. The Negro was the largest source of
          labor after all others had been ex-
          hausted.
      4. Another cause for Negroes leaving the
          South was lynching.
      5. The migration gained in momentum.
      6. Many migrants found very poor housing
          conditions in the North.

    7. Antagonism between White and
        Negro workers resulted in race
        riots.

Frederick Douglass Series:
  Six Paintings
    1. Frederick Douglass was born on
        Maryland's Eastern Shore among
        ignorant and poor Whites and
        Negro slaves.
    2. Frederick Douglass listened to
        William Lloyd Garrison denounce
        slavery.
    3. In an antislavery convention,
        Douglass and two fellow workers
        were mobbed.
    4. Douglass edited the first Negro
        paper, "The North Star."
    5. Douglas argued against John Brown's
        plan to attach the arsenal at
        Harper's Ferry.
    6. Douglass argued against poor Negroes
        leaving the South.

Toussaint L'Ouverture Series:
  Seven Paintings
    1. The birth of Toussaint L'Ouverture,
        May 20, 1743.
    2. In early manhood he was a coachman
        for Bayou de Libertas, 1763.
    3. The cruelty of the planters toward
        the slaves drove the slaves to
        revolt, 1776.
    4. Jean Francois was the first Black to
        rebel in Haiti.
    5. Toussaint captured Marmelade, held
        by Vernet, a Mulatto, 1795.
    6. General L'Ouverture, statesman and
        military genius, dreaded by the
        French, hated by the planters,
        and revered by the Blacks.
    7. Toussaint is taken to Paris and im-
        prisoned in the dungeon of the
        Castle Joux, August 17, 1802.

16. Elba Lightfoot, Painter (1910 -   )
    Portrait of a Child

17. Archibald J. Motley, Jr., Painter (1891 -   )
    Black Belt
    Old Snuff-Dipper
    Getting Religion

18. Suzanne Ogunjami (Wilson), Painter
    Full Blown Magnolia

19. Robert S. Pious, Painter (1908 -   )
    Harriet Tubman
    Portrait of Roland Hayes

20. Horace Pippin, Painter (1888 - 1946)
    Woman Taken in Adultery

21. James A. Porter, Painter (1905 - 1971)
    African Nude
    Woman Holding a Jug

22. O. Richard Reid, Painter (1898 -   )
    H. L. Mencken

23. J. H. D. Robinson, Painter (1912 -   )
    Landscape with Red Truck

24. Charles Sebree, Painter (1914 -   )
    Ethiopia's Awakening

25. Albert A. Smith, Painter (1896 - 1940)
    Ponte Vecchio
    Laughter

26. Henry O. Tanner, Painter (1859 - 1937)
    Flight into Egypt
    The Good Shepherd
    Destruction of Sodom and Gomorrah
    Christ and Nicodemus

27. Mary Lee Tate, Painter
    Morning Mist

28. Laura W. Waring, Painter (1887 - 1948)
    Portrait of a Child
    Anne Washington Derry

29. James Lesesne Wells, Painter (1902 -   )
    African Phantasy
    Composition
    The Flight into Egypt

30. Charles White, Painter (1918 -   )
    There Were No Crops This Year

31. Ellis Wilson, Painter (1899 -   )
    Charleston Sisters
    Gourds
    Old Charleston Houses
    Old Charleston Market
    Summer Magic

32. Hale A. Woodruff, Painter (1900 -   )
    Provencal Landscape
    Still Life
    The Teamster's Place

Washer Woman
The Banjo Player
Medieval Chartres
Pont Neuf
Quel de Monte Bello

Index

About the Authors

Lenwood G. Davis is an assistant professor of history at Winston-Salem State University. He received both his B.A. and M.A. degrees in history from North Carolina Central University, Durham, North Carolina, and a doctorate in history from Carnegie-Mellon University. Dr. Davis has compiled more than seventy bibliographies. He is the author of four books: *I Have a Dream: The Life and Times of Martin Luther King, Jr.,* (1973), *The Black Woman in American Society: a Selected Annotated Bibliography,* (1975), *The Black Family in the United States: a Selected Bibliography of Annotated Books, Articles, and Dissertations on Black Families in America,* (1978), and *Sickle Cell Anemia: A Selected Annotated Bibliography,* (1978). Professor Davis is presently completing two other annotated bibliographies: *Marcus Garvey,* (Janet Sims, co-author), and *Black Poets in the United States: 1747-1865.*

Janet L. Sims is reference librarian—Afro-American history specialist at the Moorland-Spingarn Research Center—at Howard University. She received her B.A. degree in sociology from North Carolina Central University, Durham, North Carolina, an M.A. degree in library science from the University of Maryland, College Park, Maryland. Ms. Sims has worked for the Library of Congress, *Congressional Quarterly,* and the Martin Luther King, Jr. Memorial Library. The compiler has had bibliographies published in the *Journal of Negro Education,* and *Black Books Bulletin.* She is the author of *Black Women in the Employment Sector,* (1979). She is presently completing three other annotated bibliographies: *Black Women in the United States, Marian Anderson,* and *Marcus Garvey* (Lenwood G. Davis, co-author).